Growing up to Salvation

John Woolmer, MA, is Rector of Shepton Mallet with Doulting in Somerset. Before his ordination he taught mathematics at Winchester College, where he subsequently became Assistant Chaplain. In 1975 he joined the staff of St Aldate's Church, Oxford, and was curate-in-charge of St Matthews, which was becoming a daughter church. He has run a number of lay training courses for city centre churches and has been involved in parish missions and renewal weekends. He is particularly interested in the churches' ministry of healing. A personal hobby is photographing, observing and breeding butterflies, an interest he shares with his wife Jane, who took the cover photograph for this book. They have three children.

JR Woolmer

Brian: may there be a superb day : Joshua 3:5

Growing up to Salvation

JOHN WOOLMER

TRi∧NGLE

First published 1983
Triangle
SPCK
Holy Trinity Church
Marylebone Road
London NW1 4DU

British Library Cataloguing in Publication Data

Woolmer, John
  Growing up to salvation.
  1. Salvation
  I. Title
  234   BT751.2

  ISBN 0–281–04070–2

Typeset by Inforum Ltd, Portsmouth
Printed in Great Britain by
The Anchor Press, Tiptree, Essex

To Jane
for her constant love, encouragement
and help

and to Rachel, Susanna
and Timothy
with the prayer that each of them is
'growing up to salvation'

Acknowledgements

My grateful thanks to the congregation of St Matthew's and St Aldate's, Oxford for their love and support. Especial thanks to those who have given me permission to mention their experiences – hopefully accurately! – and to the Community at Stanton House, where much of the book was written. Also to Anne Johnson and Joyce Martin for typing the manuscript.

Unless otherwise stated, biblical quotations are from the Revised Standard Version of the Bible, copyrighted 1946, 1952, © 1971, 1973 by the Division of Christian Education of the National Council of the Churches of Christ in the USA.

Excerpts from *Fresh Sounds* by Betty Pulkingham are reprinted by permission of Hodder and Stoughton.

Contents

Foreword

John Woolmer has already had a varied career. He discovered a living faith just before his finals at Oxford, and then taught maths at Winchester. In mid-career he left to become ordained, and returned for a further four years. After an interesting time of ministry in the school, he came to work in the quite different setting of St Aldate's, a parish church in the heart of Oxford which exercises an extensive ministry to both town and gown.

Soon he was put in charge of St Matthew's, a community church in an astonishingly mixed area across the river which had fallen on hard times. The previous incumbent, allowed just three years' independence, had begun to see real progress and under the ministry of John and Jane new shoots of life sprang up. Not all at once, nor simply as a result of preaching: but gradually through visiting, through healing, through exorcism, one here and a family there found their way to Christ. Often they came from the most bizarre of circumstances, and some of their stories are told in this book.

For salvation, in its broadest sense, is what has been happening in St Matthew's under John's ministry – and how well I recall kneeling and praying with him in that empty church the morning he took over, among the dusty pews and moth-eaten kneelers. We prayed for the church to come alive, and it has. The building has been transformed. The congregation represents a full spread in age, background, sex, intellect and outlook. They are very diverse, but they have all begun to sense the reality of the salvation of God. There is a 'wholeness' about St Matthew's – and 'wholeness' is the meaning of salvation. The church has a strong emphasis on growth, through all the ups and downs, the failures and successes.

That growth is not only in numbers, but in depth and vision. Several of the leading Christians in the congregation have not only been brought to faith out of apathy and unbelief: they have been built up, renewed by the Spirit of God, and then thrust out to work in other countries or other parts of England – just as John Woolmer himself has. So *Growing up to Salvation* is in every way a most apt title. And I am delighted to write a Foreword for a former colleage for whom I have a great respect and affection.

You will find here a very different book from anything you

have read before. John Woolmer's writing, like his preaching, is fresh and unconventional. He knows from his own wide experience the vast variety of ways in which God stoops to save a man or woman: he finds examples of most of them in the biblical stories of how different people discovered the 'wholeness' which is salvation.

But this is no dreary textbook on some dusty doctrine. It is shot through with accounts of lives John has seen brought to Christ and transformed. I worked alongside him in a number of such incidents, and can testify to God's gift of healing and deliverance, together with shrewd advice, penetrating use of Scripture, and earthy common sense which mark his ministry. He makes the examples of salvation in Bible times spring to life as he unfolds what God is doing today.

You will enjoy this book. You will learn from it. Your faith will be stimulated and your understanding deepened. Perhaps above all you will realize, as John realizes, that God cannot be put in a box, then tidily labelled and conveniently forgotten. He is the *living* God, and he is very much in business. It is his supreme concern to bring men and women to salvation, and that includes growing up to Christian maturity and fruitfulness.

My prayer is that this book will enable you to grow up to salvation. That is God's destiny for you. Don't miss it!

MICHAEL GREEN

Introduction

Some years ago, I was walking through a dark wood. I wasn't quite sure where I was going, but I had a vague desire to get through the wood and see what lay beyond. My first attempt to get out failed when the attractive sun-dappled path stopped abruptly at a tall gorse hedge. The field beyond looked inviting, the way through did not! A second route took me to the edge of a very active wasps' nest. I did a rapid U-turn back to the main path.

Eventually, after some twisting and turning, I found a path which led through the most sombre part of the wood. The trees were tall, there were no flowers, but at least the path was clear. Eventually I arrived at a gate. I climbed over it into a newly cut cornfield. The light was startlingly bright, and the sun so hot that I instinctively clung to the edge of the wood. Besides, along the edge there were blackberries and butterflies to detain me. Then I noticed some bales of straw in the centre of the field, and followed an impulse to walk towards them.

As I made my way to the centre, I suddenly realized how large the field was. It wasn't rectangular, but a huge L-shape, with the wood nestling in the crook of the L. I sat on the bales and saw that there were a number of different ways into the field. Two edges were guarded by a stream, another by the gorse hedge, the next by the brambles and a fence with my gate in it. The rest of the perimeter was lined with hedges and fencing.

There appeared to be a simple way in, which involved climbing a fence and then crossing a shallow stream. Another way, through a copse, along the edge at right angles to the wood, looked more difficult – it involved scrambling down a bank, wading through the stream and up the other side. There was also a long circuitous route through various meadows which would have led to a gate on the south side, opposite where I had entered. As I walked, I had been trying to prepare a talk for the evening (I was leading a parish house party at Blaithwaite in Cumbria). Suddenly the Lord seemed to say, 'Look at this field. I am in the centre, and there are many different ways of coming to me!'

For some, like me, it was a matter of stumbling around in the darkness of the wood, trying a number of paths, being put off by the emissaries of Satan – symbolized by the thorn hedge and the wasps – before eventually coming out of the darkest part of the wood into the brilliant light of the field. For others, there is a gentle entry, involving the crossing of shallow water, which perhaps corresponds to those who appear to grow from childhood into faith. It was a long way to the centre from that corner! Then, where the stream was deeper, there was a harder way for those who come via an experience made public by adult baptism, probably by immersion, and who then come quickly by clear steps from the edge of the field into the centre of God's love and light. Then from the south, the way was so circuitous and gentle of entry that one would hardly be aware of any particular significance of crossing into this field. This would seem to correspond to those who come very, very gently into God's Kingdom, and who perhaps only become aware of what has happened as they meet other pilgrims in the field, walking towards the centre. I suppose, too, that there are others who crash through the gorse hedge, or who are lifted through with the help of friends, who arrive battered and bruised into God's Kingdom where they begin to experience healing and freedom in the light and warmth of the field.

Everyone who enters the field has experienced the miracle of rebirth. All have been made members of God's Kingdom. But there is more to be concerned about than just entering the field. Salvation has also a present and a future tense. The field was L-shaped, and L stands for learning. God wants us to leave the shadows at the edge, and to walk boldly towards the full brightness at the centre. This is what Peter calls 'growing up into salvation' (1 Pet. 2.2). It is an exposed path and, like rabbits, we shall often prefer the shadows and the safety of the edge of the field.

Eventually, there will be a crown. Maybe, in this life, we shall not reach the bales of straw. But as we walk towards the centre, growing up into salvation, we shall have glimpses of God's glory, and become increasingly aware of other pilgrims in the field. Many people could walk in the wood, and never see one another; a few people could cling to the edge of the field and be unaware of each other; and any two walking boldly towards the centre would quickly enjoy both one another's presence and the full radiance of the sun.

1 *Learning*

'Follow me' (Mark 1.17; John 21.19).

Twice Jesus spoke these words to Peter. The first time, Peter left his job, his home, and his security, to follow the new prophet from Nazareth. Between the first call and the second lay three years of intense learning. Beyond the second call lay thirty years of leadership and service to the young Church. Service which would finally end with a martyr's death in Rome.

When Peter left his nets to follow Jesus, he became a disciple, a learner – he entered the L-shaped field.

What did Jesus expect from his disciples?

Three things in particular. Discipleship involved commitment to follow Jesus wherever he might lead. It meant growing towards spiritual maturity. And at last it would bear fruit – in character, and in evangelism.

The commitment to follow Jesus involved an immediate and sharp break with the past. Many people offered Jesus commitment on their own terms (see Matt. 8.19–22; Luke 9.57–62); this was not acceptable. Many followed when things went well, only to disappear when the opposition grew stronger.

For Peter, following Jesus involved tremendous change. Life became crowded and exciting. The very first Sabbath (see Mark 1.21–34) was extraordinary. Jesus taught with authority, exorcised a man in public, healed Peter's mother-in-law in private, and ministered to the huge crowds who flocked round the house. Hundreds were healed and set free from evil spirits; Jesus' name was on everyone's lips.

The next day, the crowds gathered again. But where was Jesus? He had gone to 'a lonely place', to pray. Eventually, Peter found him and urged him to come back. Jesus, in prayer, had discerned that God's will was to go on to other towns. The priority was to preach the coming of God's Kingdom. Peter, and the others, had to follow. Peter was beginning to learn a vital lesson; neither he, nor the crowds, could manipulate Jesus.

Over the next months, Peter followed Jesus all over Galilee. He saw multitudes fed, sick people healed, demons cast out, and the dead raised. Perhaps, for a fisherman, the subduing of

1

the sea was the most startling sight of all (Mark 4.35–41). When Jesus rebuked the wind, and said to the sea, 'Peace! Be still,' the wind ceased, and the sea became calm. The disciples were amazed. They started to ask one another, 'Who then is this, that even wind and sea obey him?'

Peter was beginning to sense the answer. When, a while later, Jesus asked the disciples who they thought he was, Peter was ready with a statement of faith: 'You are the Christ' (Mark 8.29–30).

Jesus rejoiced in Peter's inspired answer (see especially Matt. 16.17–20). He then took the opportunity to begin to warn the disciples of the hard times that lay ahead. Peter, flushed with his spiritual triumph, objected. He dared to rebuke the Master. Jesus rounded on him, accusing him of being the Devil's spokesman. From then on, the shadow of the cross hung over Jesus and his followers. There was to be no turning back. The road from Galilee was leading south towards the final climax in Jerusalem.

Gradually many of Jesus' followers disappeared, blown away, like autumn leaves in a cold wind, by the strength of the opposition. Jesus turned to the twelve (John 6.67). 'Do you also wish to go away?' he asked them. Peter relied: 'Lord, to whom shall we go? You have the words of eternal life.'

Peter had discovered that the true disciple has no alternative but to continue to follow. A true disciple is so far along the road (so clearly in the field), that to deviate or turn back is unthinkable. The initial commitment has begun to mature.

The call to follow Jesus wherever he may lead has been obeyed by all true disciples. It is tempting to think of the great examples – of Francis of Assisi renouncing riches and setting out on new paths of discipleship; of John Wesley going out into the fields and evangelizing a nation; of Dietrich Bonhoeffer deliberately returning to Germany to oppose the Nazi tyranny; of Mother Teresa following Christ's lead to serve the poorest in India. But to write only of these is to miss the point. The call to discipleship is not confined to an élite few; it comes to us all. We are either disciples or we are nothing. We are learning or we are dying. We are bearing fruit or we shall be rejected. There is no middle way.

I was greatly impressed, early in my ministry, by an elderly clergyman who, though obviously in great pain at the time, had insisted on seeing me. Lying awkwardly on his side, he asked me about my future plans, encouraged me and prayed for me. Even in his illness, he radiated the love and concern of Christ. At an age when many would retire, he had taken charge of an empty church. By the time he left it was filling up and a few years later was the only full church in the town. I met him again at a clergy retreat. He wanted to know about the renewal movement. Some aspects of it puzzled him, but his sons were involved, and even in his old age he wanted to learn. He seemed to have the ability to hear God's voice and to follow, in every situation.

Then there was a young mother, who was living with, but not married to, the father of her only child. Quite unexpectedly, she heard about Jesus from a neighbour and was converted. Immediately there was a clash of loyalties. Could she go on living, unmarried, with her son's father? She obeyed Christ, and her partner left the home. But they remained friends. He was impressed by the changes in her. Slowly and thoughtfully, he began to ask questions. Eventually he, too, became a Christian. After a period of marriage guidance counselling, they became engaged. Her obedient discipleship, and his response have probably secured their family's happiness.

A successful young executive presented his third child for baptism. For him this was to be another routine encounter with the Church. For his wife, it was a time of sadness as he had opted out of the religious upbringing of his children and left it to her. To his surprise, from the first interview the young father found himself facing his own lack of commitment. He realized that this was an important matter for himself and his whole family. He was deeply challenged by the baptismal vows: 'Do you turn to Christ? Do you repent of your sins? Do you renounce evil?' His clear replies were no routine answer, but the first signs of new life. He went out of the church with a new sense of belonging. He didn't know that it would soon lead to much practical service, to a home opened for Christian hospitality, and to leadership of a boy's organization in the church. Later he would experience three clear healings in the family (see Chapter 5). His discipleship has changed many of his former priorities.

A woman in her late thirties was suddenly convinced that God was calling her to be a nun. Unmarried, continually in pain from a back disorder, she longed for some real purpose and meaning in her life. She consulted her local vicar, who happened to be a near neighbour, and was somewhat surprised to discover that she couldn't just pack her bags and walk into a convent. For one thing, she knew little about the faith (although she had discovered something of God through her solitary quest in Bible reading and prayer). Furthermore she didn't even belong to a church, and she found it hard to relate to other people.

Slowly, all that changed. She came to know Jesus, to hear his voice and to see her prayers answered. She discovered the church and made many friends. She faced considerable opposition at home, but received a wonderful gift from God when her father had a very serious heart operation. She knew that, if she was laid up, her family wouldn't be able to cope. Just at this time of potential stress, her back was completely healed (to the delight and surprise of her osteopath!).

Eventually, to the dismay of some and the surprise of others, she felt that her call was to join a closed order. The fateful day came and she left the church and her new-found friends. Then disaster struck. Within a few days she discovered that she had made a mistake. Now she had to face the embarrassment of meeting again her family, friends and vicar. After a period of readjustment she has settled down to a job in the community and more effective service in the church. Meanwhile, she is testing out a new vocation with an open order of nuns. Full of faith, relaxed as never before, she awaits God's next directions.

A young married man with two small children became convinced that God was calling him and his wife to be missionaries. Formidable obstacles lay ahead. He needed to be accepted for training and to find financial support. The local church agreed to back him for two years. He and his family continued to live in a small, cramped community house in order to ease the financial burden. They started to learn Spanish in anticipation of being sent to do 'church planting' in Chile. The Falklands war changed all that. The British missionaries in Argentina had to leave and were sent to Spanish-speaking Chile, filling all the available posts. Our couple had to switch to learning Portuguese and to prepare for service in Brazil. Despite these and other setbacks, they cheerfully look forward to bringing up their family on the other side of the world.

Five very different sets of people in five different situations. The common factor is that in each case they have been willing,

4

like Peter, to follow Christ wherever he leads and however difficult the task seems.

The second requirement for discipleship is a willingness to learn and a desire to grow spiritually. 'Like newborn babes, long for the pure spiritual milk, that by it you may grow up to salvation,' Peter wrote in later life (1 Pet. 2.2).

Peter had learnt much about growing up to salvation. He learnt through failure. He discovered that spiritual maturity didn't involve making extravagant statements. The great boast, 'Even though they all fall away, I will not' (Mark 14.29) became the great collapse. But in that failure, Peter experienced the full forgiveness and love of Jesus. He also learnt about persecution. When next faced with opposition (Acts 4.18–22) he faced it with calm authority. His first epistle is full of strong reassurances to help his fellow Christians to stand firm in the face of fierce persecution (see 1 Pet. 4.12–19 and 5.6–11).

Peter learnt, too, from being alongside Jesus. One such learning experience was the raising of Jairus's daughter (Luke 8.40–56). Jesus, surrounded by a crowd, received an urgent message to come and pray for the daughter of the ruler of the synagogue. Hurrying to the house, on the way he felt a distinctive touch. Healing power had gone out from his body. At once he stopped and asked who had touched him. Peter, characteristically, suggested that it was an absurd question. Hundreds of people must have jostled past him. Jesus persisted and a woman with a haemorrhage came into the open. (This was important; her healing had to be witnessed by the community, otherwise she would still have been regarded as ceremonially unclean and an outcast, cf. Lev. 15.25–33.) Peter learnt the value of touch. Later (Acts 5.15) people expected to be healed if even his shadow fell upon them!

Jesus then heard that Jairus's daughter had died, and that there was now no need for him to come. Undeterred, he went to the house, ejected the mourners, and took only Peter, James, John and the parents into the girl's room. Very quickly the wailing was replaced by rejoicing, as the little girl was restored to life. Some years later, Peter himself performed a similar miracle. The raising of Tabitha (Acts 9.36–41) has many similarities to that of Jairus's daughter.

The greatest growth point in Peter's ministry was after Jesus' resurrection. First there was the joy of encounter, then the slightly painful threefold restoration (John 21.15–23). This encounter included the prophecy of Peter's martyrdom (v.18), the second command to 'follow me', and a piece of old-style interference by Peter. 'Yes, Lord, I will follow you – but what's going to happen to him [John]?' (This question, and Jesus' enigmatic reply, caused many in the early Church to believe that Jesus would return before John died. Thus this one unnecessary question caused a great deal of alarm and difficulty as the aged apostle, John, approached death some sixty years later).

After the resurrection, and particularly after the empowering experience of Pentecost, Peter was a very different sort of disciple. He still made mistakes (Gal. 2.11 for instance), but he led the Church with courage, authority and spiritual wisdom.

Many modern disciples seem to experience a later empowering experience. Some testify to a decisive growth point in their ministries. We witnessed one such occasion on a parish house party. We were speaking about the release of the Holy Spirit in people's lives. Not necessarily as a once-for-all-time experience (it wasn't for Peter) but as one way by which God leads his people out of the shadows towards the centre of the L-shaped field. One committed Christian couple who were very challenged spent most of a day talking with my wife Jane and myself. They were faithful churchgoers, believers, leaders in a small family service, yet fearfully busy with secular things and unable to grow spiritually. But quite suddenly, they had become thirsty. They longed to drink more freely from the living water (John 6.35; Isa. 55.1).

That night they and many others came into a small upper room for prayer. Most of us had never prayed for other people in this way, but the Holy Spirit seemed to take over. The wife was suddenly filled with the Spirit. She began to pray in tongues, although she scarcely knew what was meant by such an experience, and she began to receive a measure of physical healing. Her husband received a very clear call to ordination. He responded to this very quickly, and three years later was ordained. They also discovered new spiritual gifts. They became effective as counsellors, saw some friends and relatives become Christians, and developed a completely new sort of musical ministry which greatly helped their local church.

The third mark of a disciple is that he bears fruit. Jesus was quite clear about this. At the end of the Sermon on the Mount (Matt. 7.17–20) he contrasts the good and the bad trees. The theme recurs in many parables (see Mark 4), in his comments on the barren fig tree (Mark 11.12–25) and his teaching on the vine (John 15). Time and time again, he warned that mere verbal profession (e.g. Matt. 7.21) was quite inadequate. But what did Jesus mean by fruit? What was he looking for?

The two main sorts of fruit mentioned in the New Testament are the fruit of the spirit – changed lives; and the fruit from the harvest field – evangelism.

Even a cursory reading of Acts and 1 Peter shows how Peter's life changed. In Acts, we see how effective and courageous his ministry became. In 1 Peter, we read with amazement his teaching on humility. 'Humble yourselves therefore . . .' (5.6) 'Clothe yourselves with humility . . .' (5.5) Can this be the same man who tried to stop Jesus washing his feet? Is this the loud-mouthed fisherman quick to boast and quick to interrupt? Some mighty change of character has taken place. And so it will be with all of us. Sometimes we despair, and wonder how we can ever change. Yet if we are real disciples, if we have received the Holy Spirit, then the Spirit is already doing the great work of changing us.

Sometimes this shows in quite small ways. Shortly after her conversion a woman I knew started to take far more trouble with her appearance. She began to look quite different and her attractive style was an outward sign of considerable inward change. Another, who had been noticeably undomesticated and uninterested in children, turned into a creative housewife. Her house was imaginatively furnished, and she became good with her own and other people's children. One man told me he had never been able to stop swearing. Some while later, he noticed that the habit had decreased markedly. Before my own conversion I was a fanatical bridge player. Afterwards, the game ceased to interest me. I was prepared to play, but it no longer held the same fascination.

One harvest festival, I went to preach in a church near where I lived. It was an important occasion; it was a church that I would probably be asked to lead in a few months. I remember the sermon only because at the time everything seemed so heavy and so dead. I had brought a tomato plant with me. On it were green and red tomatoes. My final point, as I struggled against increasing apathy in both me and the congregation, was

7

to ask what sort of fruit were we bearing. Green tomatoes, unripe, relatively unusable; or red ones? I discovered afterwards why the atmosphere was so heavy. A spiritualist was attending the church and clearly opposing the worship and the preaching. What I didn't discover until five years later was that that sermon made a great difference to one man. He had been a servant of the church for many years, had seen much of his service wasted, and perhaps had grown somewhat disillusioned. But then he started to want 'red' tomatoes in his spiritual life. His attitude changed. From being a rather remote figure, he became one of the warmest and most welcoming. From serving a church organization as first love, he served Christ first and discovered that the organization flourished as never before. I learnt a lesson from that as well. One can often rely far too much on feelings. It was important for me to persist, despite the atmosphere, and preach the sermon. Obedience and faithfulness are qualities that God honours.

As I think of my former parishioners, and other Christians whom I have known for some years, it is not difficult to see the fruit of the Spirit in their lives. Often one sees really big changes in lives which are becoming increasingly Christ centered.

What is much harder to measure is progress in the field of evangelism. 'The harvest is plentiful, but the labourers are few' (Matt. 9.37). 'Lift up your eyes, and see how the fields are already white for harvest' (John 4.35). 'I want you to know, brethren, that I have often to come to you in order that I may reap some harvest among you as well as among the Gentiles' (Rom. 1.13).

The only time I can remember any real stir in a deanery synod was when an Anglo-Catholic from an inner city parish talked to us on evangelism. He asked us if 'our hearts burned within us with a fire that is almost unbearable to bring the Gospel to the lost.' And sadly we had to confess that our hearts didn't.

There seem to be many reasons why there is so little fruit in this most vital area. One is a sort of creeping theology of universalism; by which I mean that we feel that in the end everyone will be saved, so that evangelism doesn't matter. Once this is conceded in the area of comparative religion it is inevitably conceded in the parish. It is certainly much easier, and more popular, to treat all one's parishioners as Christians. But this is totally to ignore most of Jesus' teaching. People often say to me, 'Oh, vicar, I'm a good Christian – I live by the Sermon

8

on the Mount'. A quick reference to the contents of the Sermon on the Mount – the two roads, the two trees, the two houses – has often opened up an interesting conversation. For many people a necessary prelude to becoming a Christian is the sharp realization that they are not!

Another reason for our inability to evangelize is a total failure to obey 1 Peter 3.15 – 'In your hearts reverence Christ as Lord. Always be prepared to make a defence to any who calls you to account for the hope that is in you, yet do it with gentleness and reverence.' Yet so few Christians are prepared! How many of us could testify to our current experience of God and the difference that it makes in our life? How many of us could argue the case for the resurrection coherently? How many of us have a sufficient understanding of the cross to explain the basic doctrines of salvation (see 1 Pet. 2.24; 3.18)?

We also lack imagination! Our efforts at evangelism can be very stereotyped. Yet each person is unique. For some it may be a question of getting them to church, for another the chance conversation over a cup of coffee, for some a dinner party with speaker, for others simply consistent friendship. The opportunities are endless. Even criticism can provide opportunities. 'I don't come to your church' one woman said to me. 'It's so full of hypocrites!' I smiled at her and invited, 'Come and make one more!' To her credit, she did for a while, but sadly she didn't keep it up.

Two of the most effective evangelists I know are always looking for opportunities. One is a well-known preacher, but he has an even more valuable gift of discerning the one person in a room or after a church service who is open to the gospel. He seems to sense the lostness and the searching in their eyes. The other is a woman whose life was rescued from all sorts of pits, and who has a deep prayer life and a real desire to win others. Her enthusiasm is infectious, and she, too, has the gift of discerning those who are seriously searching for God.

A third reason for our failure in evangelism is a failure in our prayer life. We are seldom specific in our praying and we don't seem to expect answers. The Apostles, after Peter and John had been released by the Sanhedrin, prayed for more boldness (Acts 4.23–31). They had already seen three thousand converted in one day, and they prayed for more! In my own experience, I recall two particular times of fruitful prayer. One was in Nottingham, on the last night of a Cambridge University

9

Mission. A group of about twelve of us prayed with a tremendous sense of unity and purpose. And that night there was a real breakthrough in the mission and many were converted. On a very different occasion I was sitting alone in a field in Austria, praying for a forthcoming mission in the school where I was chaplain. I saw about thirty corn stooks, and the Lord seemed to say, 'Those represent people who will be converted next term'. And I said, 'Lord, that will be marvellous!' Then I saw a thin line of stooks disappearing over the hillside, and the Lord seemed to say, 'Those represent people who will be converted in the following years!' And that is just what happened. During the mission about thirty people were clearly converted and still serve the Lord eight years later; and in the following terms, long after I'd left, a steady flow of conversions took place until for a few years the Christian group in the school numbered about a hundred.

Evangelism is the lifeblood of the Church. Nothing is more exciting than the testimony of the new convert. And no one is more likely to win others than the very new believer. We must beware any standard of discipleship which doesn't rate the fruit of evangelism as a high priority.

We, who are disciples, have been commanded to make others. 'Go out into all the world and make disciples . . .' (Matt. 28.20).

2 *Rebirth*

Many centuries ago a distinguished churchman came to Jesus. He was disturbed by what he heard. 'Do not marvel that I said to you, "You must be born anew." (John 3.7). Nicodemus certainly did marvel! He had come to see Jesus at night. He was one of the religious leaders, and it was politic to be discreet about visiting this radical new teacher. He had come already favourably impressed. He had seen, or heard about, some of Jesus' miracles and now he was coming for a quiet reassuring talk. Probably he was already looking for a middle way which would take the sting out of Jesus' radical teaching and would blend it better with conventional Phariseeism. Anyway, he came and expressed his approval of Jesus as a teacher sent from God.

Jesus answered him: 'Truly, truly, I say to you, unless one is born anew, he cannot see the kingdom of God.' No exchange of academic pleasantries, just a theological thunderbolt. As many others have been since, Nicodemus was startled by the radical simplicity of the message. Somewhat lost for words, he attempted a little joke. He implied that it was as impossible for a church leader, set in his intellectual and practical ways, to change as it was physically to re-enter the womb. But Jesus persisted, now adding a new dimension to the experience – the Spirit. 'Truly, truly, I say to you, unless one is born of water and the Spirit, he cannot enter the kingdom of God. That which is born of the flesh is flesh, and that which is born of the Spirit is spirit.'

Actually, Jesus was agreeing with Nicodemus. For men, rebirth is impossible, but with God all things are possible (see Luke 18.25–30 for a similar conversation between Jesus and Peter). Nicodemus could no more engineer his own rebirth, than he could keep all the commandments. Slowly he began to realize what Jesus was saying. Being born of water was bad enough – it would probably mean submitting to the indignity of John's baptism of public immersion. As for being born of the Spirit – 'How can this be?' Jesus answered him: 'Are you a teacher of Israel, and yet you do not understand this?' If Nicodemus, one of the religious leaders, couldn't understand this basic truth, then the whole basis of his religion was questionable. It wasn't just him that was at fault, it was the whole system!

11

Such a discovery is profoundly disturbing. Martin Luther found it so in his monastery when he discovered that God's acceptance of him required, first, faith, and not the system with which he had been indoctrinated. John Wesley discovered it, as his good works collapsed around him. He went to America to convert the Indians, but he wrote in his diary, 'Who will convert me?' A clergyman friend of mine discovered the same truth when he went to America to study the renewal movement. One of his colleagues told him, 'We're praying that nothing will happen to you!' But the American visit showed him that he, too, had been missing the vital spiritual dimension.

I remember how, as an undergraduate, I began to make this discovery. I was a faithful churchgoer, I read the Bible and prayed regularly, yet it was more like a good habit than anything else. Gradually the seriousness of some others challenged me. I consulted my local vicar who assured me that all was well and that I needn't worry. But still I was uncertain – surely there must be something more, something deeper?

In a startling allusion to the cross, Jesus continued to give Nicodemus a profound theological lesson: 'As Moses lifted up the serpent in the wilderness, so must the Son of man be lifted up, that whoever believes in him may have eternal life' (John 3.14). Jesus was referring to the familiar (to Nicodemus) story in the book of Numbers (21.4–9). The children of Israel, grumbling as ever, were being punished by being bitten by deadly serpents. God told Moses to make a bronze serpent and then to lift it up on a pole. Anyone who looked at the pole, which must have seemed like a cross, would recover. A nice medieval woodcut of the incident shows the pole in the centre, the people and the snakes all around. Most are continuing to disobey. Some are trying to run away, some are praying, some are bandaging others. And all of them are in the process of being bitten. There is a certain humour (in line with some of Jesus' parables) as snakes creep up on those who are engaged in good works or religious acts. Only a few people are obeying the simple instructions and looking at the serpent. The way of salvation is too simple for most of them.

Jesus was teaching Nicodemus that the cross will be the means of salvation and that man's part will be to look to him, crucified, for salvation. It is unlikely that Nicodemus understood much of this. Presumably he left somewhat puzzled and perplexed. He had come offering Jesus his support, and had been disturbed and even humiliated.

Scripture doesn't tell us much more about Nicodemus, but we are given two more brief pictures of the man. These two glimpses give us hope that the ruler of Israel experienced the spiritual rebirth which at first he found so puzzling and threatening.

The first is when the Pharisees had unsuccessfully attempted to arrest Jesus (John 7.45–52). Their officers, impressed by Jesus, had refused to arrest him. The Pharisees planned to do the deed themselves. Nicodemus objected: 'Does our law judge a man without first giving him a hearing and learning what he does?' The Pharisees were furious. They turned on Nicodemus. They insulted him by asking if he, too, came from Galilee, and then backed up their argument with a dubious piece of theology: 'Search [the scriptures] and you will see that no prophet is to rise from Galilee.' (Nicodemus might well have replied by asking about Jonah and Hosea, to name but two!)

The second, and final, glimpse of Nicodemus is in John 19.39. After the crucifixion, Joseph of Arimathea, a respected member of the Jewish ruling council, wanted to give Jesus a proper burial. He was a secret believer, and had made some token opposition (Luke 23.50) to the proceedings of the previous night. With commendable courage, he went to Pilate and asked permission to bury the body. He intended to use his own burial cave (thereby fulfilling Isaiah 53.9). Nicodemus also came to help, bringing a huge quantity of burial spices.

Was this the first evidence of new birth? Was this the beginning of a life of discipleship? We don't know, but Christian tradition assigns an honourable history to both Joseph and Nicodemus, and we may hope that tradition is correct.

At this point two vital questions need to be asked. How is a person born again? What are the marks of the new life?

Martin Luther's faith came alive as he read the scriptures. Suddenly it all made sense. The profound disturbance was replaced by an inner peace, as the Spirit of God opened his eyes and showed him a new way. It hadn't been easy. In many ways his conversion was very gradual. There were a number of milestones. First, despite being a monk and an acclaimed teacher, he had a profound sense of his own sinfulness. Secondly, he realized that salvation is a new relationship with God based not on any good works or intentions in man, but rather

13

upon the promises and faithfulness and gift of God. Finally, as he lectured on Romans in 1516, some seven years after his quest had begun, he realized that his own faith was indeed a gift from God and he felt assurance that he was a child of God (Romans 8.16).

John Wesley's experience was somewhat different. He, too, went through years of uncertainty. His earlier 'faith' had depended upon many good works and much discipline – things which, incidentally, were then turned to great advantage in his new life. But he knew that something was missing. In a well-known passage from his diary, for the year 1737, we read:

In the evening I went unwillingly to a society in Aldersgate where one was reading Luther's preface to the Epistle to the Romans. About a quarter before nine, while he was describing the change which God works in the heart through faith in Christ, I felt my heart strangely warmed. I felt I did trust in Christ, Christ alone, for salvation; and an assurance was given me, that he had taken away my sins, even mine, and saved me from the law of sin and death.

I don't know how the clergy friend I mentioned was converted. I do know that, after he came back from America, he not only testifed to renewal, but also told a local Baptist church that he had been reborn. His ministry was revolutionized. His church grew, and new life appeared in many people.

For my own part, my search took me back to St Aldate's, in Oxford, one May morning during my final term as an undergraduate. As I was about to disappear into the safe waters of public-school teaching, this was probably the last evangelistic sermon I would hear for many years. The preacher was Ernest Shippam, managing director of a well-known food company. He didn't preach a sermon; he told his life history. It was a story of a religious upbringing, an avoidance of real commitment to Christ, a busy life and a difficult job, drink, more drink, and a real alcohol problem. Then gradually things started to change. He had a simple prayer answered when he found himself asking for an orange squash instead of a double whisky at an airport bar. Then he hired a coach to take his employees to hear Billy Graham one evening at Harringay in 1953. 'It will do them good!' he thought. At the end of the address, when Dr Graham invited inquirers to come forward, Ernest found himself leading the way. Only later did he notice his wife beside him. His conversion revolutionized his life. Family life, previously ruined by alcohol and all its attendant disorders, was transformed. Christian priorities were introduced into the firm. Some of the work force became Christians. Ernest became a lay preacher, he ran the firm to the glory of God and he was happier than he had ever been before.

I was spellbound. I'd never heard anyone preach like that. (Almost certainly I had, but it was the old problem of 'ears they have and hear not'.) Jesus was so real to him, and so distant from me; but my heart, too, was being strangely warmed. He invited anyone from the congregation to come and talk to him, then we sang the final hymn, and I tried to escape! But you can't get out of St Aldate's in a hurry and that day I just didn't seem able to get to the door. Eventually I gave up, turned back, and went to talk to the preacher. That afternoon, on my own, I prayed a faltering prayer of commitment to Christ.

Not everyone can remember a precise moment of conversion. Jesus looked for evidence of a new life, not for moments of decision. I once talked about this with a very committed lay leader during a parish mission. He longed to see people reborn, and was greatly used to counsel and help others, but he himself had had no specific moment of conversion. Brought up in a Christian home, he had always believed. But he could remember a time as a teenager when he had consciously put Christ first in some important decision. Looking back, he regarded that as evidence of conversion and the beginning of serious discipleship.

Another way of looking at the problem (and it is a real problem to many who cannot remember a moment of conversion) is to take an analogy with childbirth. From the mother's point of view, the great moment is the child's arrival in the world. It is a wonderful, exultant moment. Labour is over, new life has begun. The growing child, however, sees it rather differently. He has early memories of life, a gradual awareness that life is important (philosophically he may even realize that he is alive!) but he has no more memory of birth than of conception. For him, the process of coming alive has been a gradual one starting nine months before birth; for the mother, there will always be the memory of a decisive moment in time.

We need both perspectives. Looked at simplistically a caterpillar is 'converted' into a butterfly. What could be more differ-

15

ent? The caterpillar's sole concern is eating and survival (which may include cannibalism if necessary), his life is camouflaged and earthbound, his movements jerky and inelegant. The butterfly has a wonderful free flight high into the sky, he is concerned to mate and to secure the future of the species, he enjoys his new beauty. Yet a biologist will tell you that a caterpillar has wings. He will show you that the apparently dead chrysalis is very much alive and that the wings are steadily forming, and that the new butterfly has the same body as the old caterpillar.

When we are converted, we still have much of the old life within us, and some of our past experiences have contributed to bringing us to where we are now. People who experience sudden conversions often reject their past – especially their parents. They often don't realize that the love, and maybe the prayers, of their parents have greatly contributed to their religious development. John Wesley's rigid 'methodism' greatly helped him after his conversion. Without the discipline of prayer, reading and a simple life style, he could never have achieved so much.

But how is a person 'born again'? Scripture, and experience, should caution us against a simple answer. It would be difficult to identify the point when Peter was born again, but that didn't stop him writing about the experience (1 Pet. 1.3, 23; 2.2). It would be impossible to say when Nicodemus was born again. On the other hand, Paul (Acts 9), the Philippian jailor (Acts 16), and the Ethiopian eunuch (Acts 8), are all obvious examples of dramatic and clear conversions.

We can, however, see a number of common threads. Prior to rebirth, there is an awareness of need and of helplessness. Paul is struck blind, the jailor terrified, the eunuch puzzled, Luther is miserable, Wesley knows he is a failure . . . Jesus taught us that, when the Holy Spirit comes 'He will convince the world concerning sin . . . because they do not believe in me' (John 16.8,9). This first work of the Holy Spirit is to show us how helpless we are, to show us our sinfulness – this was Isaiah's reaction in the Temple when given God's commission (Isa. 6); this was Peter's reaction in the boat when the fishes were landed (Luke 5.8).

Our first response is to try harder. But gradually we realize futility of the struggle. The great Chinese Christian Watchman Nee illustrated this graphically with a story of a boy drowning in a river. A strong swimmer, a Christian leader, stood on the bank doing nothing. Eventually he jumped in and saved the boy. Others remonstrated with him and said he should have gone in sooner. But the rescuer explained that he needed to wait until the boy had stopped struggling; then he could be rescued safely and easily. To have gone in earlier would have been much more difficult and potentially dangerous.

So it is spiritually. It is when we realize that we need saving, and that we cannot save ourselves, when we stop struggling, that we are ready to receive God's grace.

It is relatively easy to understand, and believe, that our sins are a fatal barrier between us and God, but it is far less easy to understand, or to accept, that the cross is God's solution to the problem (see 1 Cor. 1.18–31).

Canon Keith de Berry described in a sermon how he was travelling in a Norwegian fjord. A suspension bridge was being built from the mainland to a small island. A great arch came out from the mainland, and a tiny one from the island, and there was a gap in the middle. Then he saw a huge crane, bearing the final arc, move into position. The crane and the missing piece looked like a cross. Together they bridged the gap. That is one part of the work of the cross. The unbridgeable gulf is removed.

But even if the gulf is bridged, how can we cross it?

There is a tremendous passage in Tolkien's *The Lord of the Rings* which unconciously illustrates this. The ring bearer and his band are trapped in some deep caves. They come to a narrow bridge which will lead to safety. A fierce enemy pursues them. Gandalf, their spiritual leader, sends them over to the other side, while he fights a fatal battle with the Balrog on the bridge. He dies so that the others can escape.

Jesus cried out, 'My God, my God, why hast thou forsaken me?' (Mark 15.34); not because he had reached the end of his tether, not even as a quotation from a psalm, but because he was bearing the sins of the whole world. The sinless had become the sinbearer. Small wonder the sky darkened.

Sometimes I use a visual aid to illustrate this. Imagine a whole array of small candles burning brightly. Then watch while a jar is put over them. Very quickly the oxygen is burnt up, and the lights go out and thick black smoke whirls about. The candles cannot be relit unless the jar is removed. Alongside, there is one great big candle burning on a silver candlestick. The jar is removed and placed over the candlestick. The bright light flickers and goes out. But because the jar has been lifted from the little candles, any of them can now be lit . . .

And so it is with us. That is the heart of the gospel! Not only is the sin barrier broken, not only is the way to God open, but we can receive him into our hearts by faith. 'To all who received him, who believed in his name, he gave power to become children of God' (John 1.12).

At this point I explain that all that is necessary is a simple prayer expressing penitence, belief, and asking to receive the gift of the Holy Spirit. If the Holy Spirit has brought a person this far, it is usually pretty clear that it is right to continue. I usually make three suggestions. 'Either pray with me here and now, or go away and pray on your own, or come back in a few days and we will talk further.' (Two possible forms of prayer are given at the end of the chapter.)

Various doubts and hesitations usually surface at this point. These need gentle and sensitive handling. Forceps deliveries, inductions and Caesarean sections are quite unnecessary processes in spiritual birth. A person may say he is not ready. Often this is true, and it is most unhelpful to try to force people forward – although occasionally they need a push (Jude vv. 22,23)! A man who had experienced some physical healing, who seemed convinced intellectually, and who had seen the beginnings of change in his wife, asked me, 'Is it about time I became a Christian?' I felt it right to give him a firm push towards the Kingdom.

Some people say, 'I'm not sure if I'm a Christian.' This happens both when they've already taken a 'decision' – often long ago as a child or a teenager – and when they've had no definite conversion experience. I find that to ask them to renew their baptismal vows[1] is often very helpful. This leaves in God's hands the question of their past spiritual standing; and it gives them a decisive moment to look back to. It also gives a chance for them to confess and renounce any obvious sins which may be strangling their Christian growth.

It is very exciting to watch the birth of a butterfly. To the discerning eyes, the signs that all is ready are there. The chrysalis has darkened, the wing colours show through in miniature, the case begins to crack . . . Then quite suddenly the new-born insect emerges. Its wings are tiny; anxiously it looks for somewhere to hang. Will it survive? Then it settles and pumps the life blood into the wing cases. Visibly, they expand and then the butterfly settles down to let them dry before making the first flight. This miracle of nature takes place swiftly and efficiently. It is a dangerous time for the insect, but few seem to be damaged or lost. To the beholder, the change is mystical and never fails to excite.

It is a far more wonderful experience to be present when someone's heart is opened to receive the Holy Spirit (Acts 16.14). Yet it is strangely tempting to be doubtful. Has anything happened? Did they feel anything? Will it last? Will they? . . . Nearly always these fears are groundless. Often the person seems immediately different – the eyes become clear, the face relaxes. On other occasions they come back a few days later full of joy and of new experiences, the miracle of rebirth has begun!

Which brings us to a last and most important question. What are the marks of new life? A genuine Christian will be hungry for worship, will want to be taught, will have some experience of God in prayer, will enjoy reading the Bible. Many new believers receive wonderful answers to prayer. God seems especially to encourage us in those early days. It is thrilling to hear a new Christian speak of new discoveries and experiences.

My friend Sue was very doubtful about her conversion – especially about the need for repentance. After a very tentative commitment to Christ, her minister advised her to go home and pray. This she did, hardly knowing where to start, by telling God about all the doubts that were besetting her. The matter of repentance was a major block. She felt she did not really need to repent, as she wasn't to blame for her unruly past (beaten up by her mother, a tennis career unfulfilled because of a motorcycle accident . . .).

At this point a strange phrase came into her mind, 'Romans three twenty-three'. She had no idea what it meant – all she could think of was 323 Roman soldiers. But for a whole week this phrase haunted her. Eventually she realized that it might have something to do with the Bible; but as she hadn't got a Bible, she was somewhat stuck. She confided in the friend who had first taken her to church – and the mystery was soon unravelled: Romans 3.23: 'All have sinned and fall short of the glory of God.' Sue knew then that God was speaking to her about repentance. *All* had sinned – herself included!

The most amazing thing, to her, was that God, whom she hardly knew, could speak to her through the Bible, which she had never read. She has never since doubted the authenticity and authority of Scripture, and has many times been given equally telling references for other people.

Another major factor in Sue's conversion was the prayers of her friends who first took her to church. They prayed specifically for the block between her and God to be removed. Paul writes about the veil over the mind of the unbeliever (2 Cor. 3.12—4.6). When we pray for an unbeliever, we are praying that this veil will be lifted. This brings the person into the presence of God – but he is still free to accept or reject God's call. We are commanded to pray (see Rom. 10.1, 14–17), but the results of such prayer rest between God and the individual.

The other major result of new birth is – love. 'We know that we have passed out of death into life, because we love the brethren' (1 John 3.14). A colleague of mine, visiting on a caravan estate, found a man who claimed to have been born again years ago, but was quite happy in total spiritual isolation and claimed not to need anyone else. Sadly, too, some of the things that 'born again' politicians say don't sound particularly loving, and help to discredit such theology in the eyes of thoughtful citizens.

On the other hand, the genuine believer senses a new belonging, a new identity, especially among Christian friends. My wife, Jane, experienced this. She was quite lonely as a student in London. Then she became a Christian and found herself surrounded by new friends.

The new disciple will also have his eyes opened to the needs of the world. His attitude to the deprived, to the homeless, the unemployed, those of different racial origin, will change radically. Many very young Christians give effective service overseas with missions or aid agencies. Others seek out the less privileged in their own country. They are responding to St John's penetrating words: 'He who does not love his brother whom he has seen, cannot love God whom he has not seen.' (1 John 4.20)

One marvellous 'plus' is a sense of purpose. Life to the newly born no longer seems meaningless, but offers endless opportunities for service and testimony. There is an ancient version of the Bible which says, 'God was with Jacob and he was a lucky fellow!' This new sense of purpose brings plenty of surprises. I, for one, never dreamed that becoming a Christian might eventually mean being ordained. Perhaps that is just as well, or I might have fought a little harder to get out of St Aldate's that

Sunday and never have stayed to talk with Ernest Shippam!

And now the warning! After the call, there is a cost. Luke 14.27: 'Whoever does not bear his own cross, cannot be my disciple. For which of you, desiring to build a tower, does not first sit down and count the cost, whether he has enough to complete it? Otherwise, when he has laid a foundation, and is not able to finish, all who see it begin to mock him, saying "This man began to build, and was not able to finish".'

The cost will become clearer later in this book. At the very least it involves loss of independence; it may involve mockery from erstwhile friends and family; in some countries it may involve real persecution and loss of livelihood. We do a great disservice to potential disciples if we do not warn them about this. Life will be far more difficult, but their resources will be far greater, and they will never regret it.

With the cost, there is also a crown. The crown of Christ. His love, his friendship, and his strength!

Here are two possible prayers of commitment. The first is for the complete newcomer to Christ, and the second for the one who is not sure. The prayers are offered as a pattern.

'Lord Jesus, thank you for calling me. Please give me a real desire to repent. Show me any particular sins that need to be forsaken. Grant me a sense of what my sin has cost you, a deepening appreciation of your saving work, and faith in your resurrection. And Lord, having brought me to the foot of your cross, please wash me clean from my sin, and may I receive your Holy Spirit. Come Lord Jesus that I may be born again, and enter into the inheritance that you have prepared for me.'

'Lord Jesus, in your name I renounce evil. I repent of my sins and in particular ask for your help to set me free from . . . I turn to you, in penitence and faith, and ask that henceforward I may be your faithful soldier and servant, cleansed by your blood and led by your Spirit.'

NOTE
1   The baptismal vows are to be found in the Alternative Service Book, p. 276. They are: 'I turn to Christ . . . I repent of my sins . . . I renounce evil.' There then follow three affirmations of belief.

3 *Forgiveness*

A woman once shared with me how, some years earlier, her father had committed suicide by hanging. She felt guilty and unable to forgive herself. I was able to tell her that she was talking to someone who understood, because I had had a similar experience. I assured her that God didn't want her to live imprisoned in the past, but to receive his forgiveness now, and to move forward free from guilt and self-reproach: 'Whether or not you were partly to blame – and I don't suppose you were – is irrelevant. God wants to free you now.' Then I prayed for her, laying my hands on her head and quoting verses of Scripture such as 'You will know the truth, and the truth will set you free' (John 8.32). At this she began to cry, but the tears were tears of joy. She explained afterwards that, when I laid hands on her, she saw a picture of a rope snapping. She was free at last.

As I shared her joy, I marvelled at the strange ways of God. The lowest point of my life, the time of my father's death, had been of help to someone else. Several times since, God has brought me back to this experience in order to help others. As the Psalmist puts it (Ps. 84.6): 'Blessed is the man . . . who going through the vale of misery uses it for a well.' [BCP]

Many people, like this woman, feel blocked from receiving God's peace by a deep sense of guilt and shame. This is particularly so where there has been some sexual sin. Painful though it is, they need to talk about it, confess it, receive prayer, and then really believe that the past can be buried. The symbolism of baptism is important here, expressing the reality of the burial of the past, and the rising cleansed to new life. Sometimes it is helpful for people to renew their baptismal vows (see Ch. 2). We need continually to stress that God is far more concerned with how we are treating our neighbour today, than with youthful indiscretions of twenty years ago.

Others, on the contrary, sense little need of God's forgiveness. They may have sharply defined categories of sin (theft, violence, immorality . . .) which they have not knowingly committed, and so they feel they are in the clear. Jesus once told a parable to illustrate this point; 'A certain creditor had two debtors; one owned 500 denarii, the other 50. When they could not pay, he forgave them both. Now which of them will love him the more?' (Luke 7.41–2). The meaning of this parable was clear. Jesus was a dinner guest in the house of Simon, a Pharisee. In the middle of the meal, a woman, described as a sinner (which almost certainly means that she was a prostitute), came and stood behind him weeping. Then she covered his feet with her tears, kissed them and anointed them with oil. Simon was shocked by this behaviour. Jesus, on the other hand, recognized that the woman was deeply ashamed of her past, and saw her actions as a parable of true repentance towards God. He pronounced that not only was she forgiven, but that her act of faith had saved her. Simon had done little for Jesus. He had not even offered the traditional welcoming ceremonies to his guest. He probably didn't even notice that in Jesus' story the debtor who owned 50 denarii couldn't pay either!

It is always deeply moving to meet people who have a tremendous sense of God's forgiveness. As it happens I have met several full-time Christian workers who first encountered God in prison. Their gratitude is deep and their testimony powerful. Ex-drug addicts, alcoholics, and failed suicides who have become Christians usually have a wonderful sense of God's love and an almost euphoric sense of joy.

A former colleague told me how two priests, both alcoholics, were on retreat with their bishop. The bishop, a discerning man, when he had heard their confessions, acted decisively. Laying hands on each of them, he prayed for their complete freedom. When they got home, one telephoned the other. They found themselves laughing as they shared their experiences of deliverance. One question arose – what to do with their not inconsiderable stocks of alcohol? The answer was simple! One loaded his crates of bottles into his car and drove round to his friend's vicarage. Bottle by bottle, with much hilarity, they poured the stuff away. Each time they flushed the loo, there was a renewed cry of 'Praise the Lord.' Two parish ministries were subsequently much transformed.

The apostle Paul was someone who was forgiven much. He could never forget that he had once persecuted the Church (1 Cor. 15.9; 1 Tim. 1.15); he could never forget seeing Stephen die. He knew how completely he had opposed the true purposes of God. The blindness which accompanied his conversion was a poignant reminder to him of his spiritual state. If his penitence was deep, his gratitude to God was deeper.

23

Those of us who have sinned less (and there are degrees of sin), though concious that we couldn't pay our debt, are sometimes almost envious of those who have so obviously received so much. It is very easy to behave like the elder brother in the parable (Luke 15.25–32) and fail to appreciate God's goodness to us.

Yet we all can expect to receive deep experiences of forgiveness even though our sins may be more subtle. Only once have Jane and I sought marital counselling. Nothing particular was wrong, but nothing in particular was right. We spent half an hour with Colin Urquhart, who gently showed us areas where we were expecting too much of each other and taking each other for granted. The sense of relief and joy afterwards was enormous. I felt as though I was walking on air. God seemed very gracious and very forgiving. As we were back in Blaithwaite at the time we went to the L-shaped field for a celebration walk.

On a sadder occasion, I was conscious of inadvertently contributing to a young man's mental breakdown. He was convinced that he was possessed by demons. After doing everything that I could to explore the possibility, I felt able to assure him that this wasn't the problem. But then unthinkingly I took him to a household where some strange psychic things were happening. This caused him to 'flip'. He had to go into a mental hospital and over a period of years has made an encouraging improvement. I felt partly responsible and very guilty. Gradually I was able to receive God's forgiveness. In particular this involved realizing that I must release to God the burden of ministry. He had to teach me that we cannot always succeed, and we need to be released from the consequences of our ministry. If we give God the glory for the successes, we must allow him to bear the shame of the failure. But the sense of forgiveness in this incident was completed by the boy's father. He made it clear throughout that he didn't blame me, and continued to offer me his friendship, and to consult me about his son and other situations. I was deeply grateful to him.

It is often true that forgiveness isn't complete until we are ready to receive the forgiveness of man, as well as of God. This is particularly painful in church or family relationships. Occasionally, particularly after divorce, such forgiveness is not available. David (2 Sam. 11) could never receive the forgiveness of Uriah the Hittite. He had stolen his wife, organized his death, and now he couldn't even ask for his forgiveness!

In such situations, we are tempted to feel that forgiveness is impossible. David's deep understanding of God's nature helped him through the situation. While the child of the union lay sick, his remorse and penitence were very deep. When the child died (2 Sam. 12.19) his servants were afraid to tell him. They were sure that he would go completely wild. But David sensed what had happened, received the news calmly, and stopped grieving. He had received God's punishment, and now he was forgiven. His life returned to a more or less even keel.

Sexual sins often bring about particular problems. People may be deeply troubled about sins which have occurred years earlier. It is strange how hard it is to discover a balanced biblical position on these matters. Christian people seem either to be paralyzed with guilt or full of self-justification. Counselling and prayer can bring relief, not only from the guilt but to the problem itself. I have seen, for instance, a few people with deep homosexual problems completely released and eventually living a normal married life.

The Bible neither magnifies nor glosses over sexual problems. Such sins are not unforgivable, neither are they unimportant. Jesus' treatment of the woman taken in adultery (John 8) displays compassion, realism and firmness. He showed great compassion to the woman, great realism when he challenged any Pharisee without sin in these matters to cast the first stone, great firmness when he sent the woman away with the words, 'Go, and sin no more'.

Some situations do present formidable problems. What do you say to a mother who confesses to having killed her baby years earlier? (I once had to support a rather shattered counsellor who had received this confession.) What do you say to a swindler who has robbed hundreds of people and has no means of finding them even if he had the money to repay them? What do you say to someone with burning hatred towards a dead parent? What do you say to a Christian leader who tells you that he is soon to be the father of an illegitimate child? What do you say to a man who has confessed sexual malpractice to his wife, and now she can't trust him? What do you say to a violent husband who just cannot control his anger in certain situations?

Two verses of Scripture are very relevant here: 'Come now, let us reason together, says the Lord, though your sins are like scarlet, they shall be white as snow, though they are red like crimson, they shall become like wool' (Isa. 1.18). He who comes to me, 'I will in *no wise* cast out' (John 6.37 AV).

Sometimes it helps the penitent to say these verses out loud. It is not 'he who comes with perfect faith', or with a good character, or with no past; but simply he who *comes* to me, 'I will in *no wise* cast out'. In these deep situations, Scripture binds up the broken hearted, and releases the captives in ways that no earthly counsellor can match.

The absence of any true sense of guilt is more difficult to cope with. Like Simon the Pharisee, many of us can be remarkably self-righteous, even if we do not go as far as the Duchess of Buckingham who replied to a letter from the Countess of Huntingdon, one of the leaders of the eighteenth century Methodist movement:

I thank your ladyship for the information concerning the Methodist preachers: their doctrines are most repulsive, strongly tinctured with impertinence and disrespect towards their superiors, in perpetually endeavouring to level all ranks and do away with all distinctions. It is quite monstrous to be told that you have a heart as sinful as the common wretches that crawl on the earth. This is highly offensive and insulting and I cannot but wonder that your ladyship would relish any sentiment so much at variance with high rank and good breeding.

The indignation of certain politicians of our own day over the Falklands War thanksgiving service in St Paul's Cathedral has some of the same touches. It is necessary for us, as Christians, to forgive our enemies and pray for them. It is also necessary for us as members of a nation at war to acknowledge some corporate responsibility for the war. Some expression of guilt was therefore highly appropriate.

Parish visiting has taught me that most ordinary people today have little sense of sin. They regard themselves as Christians. They were christened, attended Sunday School, send their children there, 'have never done any harm', say their prayers (when in trouble), and believe in God. Any idea that they might need God's forgiveness seems absurd when our social standards condone all manner of sin, the psychiatrists tell us it isn't our fault, and frequently the Church agrees with them. Talk about sin seems offensive to many people, and Jesus irrelevant. How right Paul was (2 Cor. 4.3–4); 'Our gospel . . . is veiled only to those who are perishing. In their case the god of this world has blinded the minds of unbelievers, to keep them from seeing the light of the gospel of the glory of Christ.'

A nice example of this sort of blindness was provided by a prisoner in Winchester gaol. A friend of mine was talking to him about capital punishment. He was all in favour of it. My friend gently reminded him that he was in prison for murdering his wife. 'Oh that was just a little domestic difficulty', the man replied.

Paul analyzes his own experience of spiritual blindness in Romans 7. He too was convinced that he was righteous until suddenly he was convicted by the tenth commandment. He realized that he coveted all sorts of things and that he, too, was guilty of breaking the law.

The Christian gospel is not merely the best religious option, or the way to self-fulfilment, or to life at its best. The apostolic preaching told men plainly that they were sinners in the sight of God and needed to repent. It is possible that our attitude to confession in church and in our pastoral work may encourage people to forsake small sins without ever showing them the sort of total lifegiving repentance that God is looking for.

How can we be brought to repentance? Large texts and gloomy countenances don't help. (My mother used to enjoy telling how she followed a lorry with PREPARE TO MEET THY DOOM printed in large letters on its back door. Eventually, its driver signalled her to overtake – just as a car came fast in the opposite direction!) Prayer, and faithful preaching, have brought results in the past. All the great revivals, such as those under Whitefield and Wesley, began with deepening of a sense of sin. Tears, loud groanings, and long spiritual battles feature frequently in accounts of revival meetings in those days.

Sometimes God uses quite simple things to bring this vital conviction of sin. As an undergraduate, about a year before my conversion, I worked in a factory on a scheme connected with the South London Industrial Mission. I felt very virtuous at giving up a month of my vacation to discover how the other half lived. One of the other undergraduates on the scheme was not a Christian, but her social concern, and general behaviour, put me to shame. I believe she did a lot to puncture my feelings of self-righteousness and to prepare the way for conversion.

True repentance has two aspects. It involves seeking as far as possible to put the past right, and turning to God's way in the future. The story of Zaccheus (Luke 19) is a perfect example. Jesus was walking through Jericho; an excited crowed thronged around him. They had already witnessed the healing of the blind man. Doubtless they were looking for more miracles. Jesus, by contrast, was looking for a particular man. Just as he had known the precise needs of many other people, so he knew Zaccheus by name and by repute.

Zaccheus was determined to see Jesus. He went to considerable trouble, and risked some embarrassment to do so. It must have amused the onlookers to see this rich swindler going through the indignity of climbing a tree. Like the bishops and noblemen who hid behind curtains in fashionable houses to hear John Wesley preach, Zaccheus doubtless felt both conspicuous and uncomfortable.

Jesus' gaze penetrated the leaves of the tree. His command was clear: 'Zaccheus, make haste and come down; for I must stay at your house today.' Suddenly Zaccheus was exposed to the view of the crowd and to the full majesty of Jesus. Without time to think, he scrambled down the tree. The silent onlooker had become the centre of attention.

Zaccheus went home and received Jesus joyfully. The people were upset. Didn't Jesus realize how he extracted excessive taxes from rich and poor alike and kept the balance for himself? And now, he was accepting his hospitality; apparently vindicating this nasty little man and his unpleasant trade. They missed, or ignored, the point that Jesus was displaying most clearly the compassion and insight of God. They criticized (as we often do) without waiting to find out.

For Zaccheus, the whole object of the visit was becoming gloriously clear. He knew what he had done, he knew to whom it had been done, and he knew what to do. What followed was an acted parable of true repentance. 'Behold, Lord, the half of my goods I give to the poor; and, if I have defrauded anyone of anything, I restore it fourfold.' This was no cheap way to grace, no easy repentance. Not only were the financial implications considerable, but the cost of facing those whom he had swindled was much greater. How much easier to have said, 'Behold Lord all my goods, I have given away.' Although this would have stripped him financially, it would have protected him from the embarrassing business of saying 'sorry' to those whom he had hurt.

People can be remarkably unimpressed by apparent repentance. Recently a Sunday newspaper carried a cynical piece about a British businessman who had left the country, leaving behind a collapsed company, and who had become a 'born again' preacher in America. Chuck Colson, and others converted post-Watergate, have doubtless faced hostile reactions to their change of lifestyle. Of course, such scepticism is sometimes justified. Paul puts the options clearly in 2 Corinthians 7.10: 'For godly grief produces a repentance that leads to salvation and brings no regret, but worldly grief produces death.' Zaccheus waited for Jesus' verdict on his repentance. Jesus gave it clearly and unequivocally: 'Today salvation has come to this house, since he also is a son of Abraham.'

There was a certain irony in this reply. Not only was Zaccheus forgiven, but also he was a true son of Abraham. Jesus had offended apparently believing Jews by telling them they were not Abraham's children in any real spiritual sense (John 8.34–47). Now he declared this miserable collaborator a true son of the father of the Jewish nation.

Such is the extent of God's forgiveness and restoration. God's grace is sufficient to forgive anyone anything.

I have a favourite visual illustration of repentance. I turn my back on my visitor and start talking to the wall. After a while, I turn my head and ask him if he is still there. He laughs uncertainly. Eventually I turn right round, face him, and explain. 'I've been doing what we all do to God. We go our own way. We talk to him on our own terms. Occasionally, especially when in trouble, we turn round and see if he's still there. But what he requires from us is quite different. He wants us to go completely his way. That's what repentance means.' And when you've done that, God gives you his Holy Spirit to make the change possible (to be more precise it is the Holy Spirit who has brought you this far, though you don't realize it!). It's not essentially up to you, it's up to him, to keep you in the changed state. Such total repentance will inevitably, like Zaccheus', include restitution and penitence. And it is lasting and life-giving. 'If we confess our sins, he is faithful and just, and will forgive our sins and cleanse us from all unrighteousness' (1 John 1.9).

Some people think that ultimately forgiveness is inevitable

for everyone, regardless of their attitude. They will quote texts to support such a view: ('God desires all men to be saved and come to the knowledge of the truth' (1 Tim. 2.4). 'The grace of God has appeared for the salvation of all men' (Titus 2.11). 'For God has consigned all men to disobedience, that he may have mercy upon all' (Rom. 11.32). This view presents God as an eternal chess player who by his persistent love must win every game. His enduring patience will checkmate our sin and bring all mankind forgiveness.

It sounds very attractive – but is it true? The balance of Scripture, and (less importantly) experience, say a clear 'no'. The whole thrust of Jesus' ministry was that people must *choose*. They were for him or against him, on the narrow road or the broad, wheat or tares, good fruit or bad, wise virgins or foolish . . . The basic theme of John's Gospel is the contrast between light and dark, between sight and blindness. There is nothing to indicate that all will walk in the light. Indeed that tragic moment when Judas leaves the last supper, 'and it was night' (John 13.30), implies the exact opposite.

The cross becomes tragically unnecessary if everyone is to be saved in the end. We don't need to think of the extreme cases, like Hitler or Stalin, to see the implications. Think of an atheist friend railing, on his death bed, against religion, or of a relative who firmly declared that he didn't want to go to heaven: 'There'd be no bridge, no sex, and only music which I can't stand!' Will God violate the free and clear choice made by such people?

God's forgiveness has two conditions. The first is the fairly obvious one that we receive it and act upon it. Zaccheus and the woman who disturbed Simon's supper party did both. Eternal life is the gift of God (Rom.6.23). But what if we don't want the gift? 'I have come that they may have life and have it abundantly' (John 10.10). But what if we don't want his life? 'The Son of Man came to give his life as a ransom for many' (Mark 10.45). But what if we don't want a ransom paid for us? (Obstinate people sometimes go to jail rather than pay a fine and beseech their friends not to pay the fine.) God's offer of forgiveness is free – but we have to respond.

The other condition is that, to be forgiven, we have to forgive others. 'Forgive us our sins, as we forgive those who sin against us', we pray in the Lord's Prayer. 'If you do not forgive men their trespasses, neither will your Father forgive your trespasses'. (Matt. 6.15) The parable of the unforgiving servant ends with the solemn warning: 'So also my heavenly father will do to everyone of you, if you do not forgive your brother from your heart.' (Matt. 18.35) 'And whenever you stand praying, forgive, if you have anything against anyone; so that your Father who is in heaven may forgive you your trespasses.' (Mark 11.25)

A classic example of the difficulty of obeying this injunction is given by Lord Egremont in his amusing book *Wyndham and Children First*. He noticed a fellow civil servant looking very puzzled and asked him what the trouble was. The man explained that, when at school, he had been very bullied. In particular, he suffered from claustrophobia. One day his chief tormentor had shut him inside a trunk. The tormentor had just written to him asking for forgiveness. Apparently he had become a clergyman and was dying and wished to put his affairs right. The civil servant – a fearfully honest man – went through agonies and eventually sent a telegram 'Sorry – cannot forgive'.

Corrie Ten Boom tells how, after the war, she was called to preach a message of forgiveness and reconciliation. Most of her family, including her beloved sister Betsie, had been killed by the Germans. She had been imprisoned in Ravensbrück and in other camps. She told the Lord she would go anywhere – except Germany. The Lord directed her to Germany! One evening, after she had been preaching about forgiveness, a German walked forward. She recognized him as one of the SS officers from the camp where her sister had died. He, of course, didn't recognize her. He held out his hand. He told her he had become a Christian since the war, and that he would like to receive her forgiveness. She couldn't do it. It was impossible. Yet wasn't this the basis of her preaching? Didn't God love the unlovable and forgive the unforgivable? She prayed. A current of warmth passed down her shoulders to her hands, she embraced him. Forgiveness and reconciliation for both of them was complete.

Fred Smith, the Oxford evangelist, told me how at one of his public healings meetings, a woman and her husband came forward together for prayer. He was about to pray for them when the Holy Spirit said, 'Don't. She hasn't forgiven her husband.' Somewhat nonplussed, but obedient as ever, Fred shared this with the woman. 'Oh yes,' she said, 'that's quite true. I haven't forgiven my former husband.' She was then able to say a prayer of forgiveness, and after that to receive ministry for healing.

I've met several people with a deep problem of this kind – particularly towards parents. Sometimes this bitterness seems to have caused actual disease. Often in such cases forgiveness can only by undertaken gradually and gently. Years of hurt cannot be dispelled in one superficial prayer. A first stage may be to tell God that you are willing for him to make you able to forgive. This confession lets in a chink of light and seems to allow the Holy Spirit to begin a work of healing.

Sometimes the gift of knowledge (1 Cor. 12.8) can unlock an unexpected hurt from the past. Jesus' gentle exposure of the woman of Samaria's past is an example (John 4). Once, two of us were praying for a girl, part of whose problems seemed to stem from a Jehovah's Witness upbringing. We felt that this was an area needing forgiveness and healing. The girl was rather sceptical. My colleague Elizabeth saw a picture of a thorn hedge. At first, this made no sense, and we were inclined to forget it. Then the girl remembered! The Jehovah's Witness minister was always preaching about thorn hedges. Here was a simple confirmation that our ministry was in the right area.

A West Indian member of our congregation in Oxford one day told me with some embarrassment, 'John, I must share something with you. All the time you've been here I haven't been able to listen to your sermons because I can't stand your voice. I'm sorry!' I laughed, accepted his apology, and we became good friends. Confession and mutual forgiveness unlocked a relationship.

Quite small things like that can easily spoil our fellowship and prevent growth. How easy it is to be irritated by people's habits – even by their method of praying! – and we need to let go of such things quickly. It is amazing how some people hold on to hurts for years. They are never brought out into the open, just left to fester.

Clergy are particularly vulnerable here. People so easily take offence! We forget their names, fail to appreciate their help, get distracted when talking to them, fail to visit them when sick (often because we aren't told) . . . We must encourage our congregations to forgive and forget.

If someone comes and tells me about a problem he has with a third person I always try to get the two together. It may be painful, but it is certainly worth it (and it follows the clear and usually ignored teaching of Jesus in Matthew 18.15–20).

I wonder whether Simon the Pharisee ever managed to forgive the sinful woman for breaking into and disturbing his dinner party.

4 *Faith*

'Stop doubting and believe' (John 20.27 NIV).

Poor Thomas! He is remembered only for his great confession of doubt. He wasn't even the only one of the eleven who doubted (Matt. 28.17), but his declaration was bolder, more emphatic, and more memorable.

'Unless I see in his hands the print of the nails, and place my finger in the mark of the nails, and place my hand in his side, I will not believe' (John 20.25). Thomas was going to take plenty of convincing. The others had seen something – a ghost, an apparition, perhaps even an angel; *that* he might believe – but he required much clearer evidence before he was convinced by this talk of resurrection. He needed to see the marks of the crucifixion and to touch the wounds.

Thomas seems to have been of a naturally gloomy disposition. Faith comes harder to those for whom life seems difficult. Twice, in the gospels, he exhibited a touch of despondency. On the first occasion, Jesus had just told the disciples that their friend Lazarus had died (John 11.14). He had intimated that something rather special was going to take place, but Thomas didn't pick up the nuance. Grimly he said, 'Let us also go [to Jerusalem], that we may die with him.' Jesus had already been warning the group that real trouble lay ahead. Now one of their most reliable friends had died. Thomas caught the mood, and suggested that they might as well go to Jerusalem and get the business of dying over with. What Thomas made of the Lazarus miracle is not recorded.

A little while later (John 14), Jesus started to speak of his own impending death. He spoke of comfort and of hope. He assured his disciples that he was going on ahead, and that he would prepare a place for them. 'You know the way to the place where I am going.' Encouraging words for most, but not for Thomas! 'Lord, we don't know where you are going, so how can we know the way?' [NIV]

This is the devastating logic of depression. It is one of its most difficult characteristics that words which are meant to encourage seem just to add to the blanket of gloom. If we are cheerful, it is an unbearable contrast to our friends' depression. If we are

34

miserable, this adds more reasons for their despondency.

People who suffer from depression seem to have the knack of being in the wrong place at the wrong time. A depressed person comes to a healing service on the night that few are healed. A depressed person, seeking to help someone else, turns up at an unhelpful moment, and feels rejected. So it was with Thomas. He just *had* to be missing when Jesus walked through the locked doors and encouraged the other ten with the wonderful experience of his resurrection! But Thomas didn't have to wait long. A week later, Jesus came again. Graciously, he fulfilled all Thomas's pre-conditions. Mary Magdalen (John 20.17) had not been allowed to touch him; Thomas was. Gently but firmly, Jesus rebuked him. 'Stop doubting and believe.' Thomas obeyed. Overwhelmed, he responded, 'My lord and my God!'

Throughout Christian history, there have been a small number of people who have been converted through a sudden experience of meeting the Risen Christ. Eldridge Cleaver, a leading member of the Black Panthers, tells in his autobiography, *Eldridge Cleaver: Ice and Fire*, of an experience in which Christ appeared to him. Desperate, on the run from the law in the United States, he had fled to France. He stood on a balcony looking at the stairs and thought about killing himself. He looked at the shadows on the moon, which resembled a sort of man, and saw successively images of himself on a Black Panther poster, then of his political heroes Castro, Mao, Marx, and then suddenly Jesus Christ. He was terrified. When he looked at Christ's eyes, he began to shake uncontrollably. Trembling and crying he managed from ancient memory to recite the Lord's Prayer and the Twenty-third Psalm. The next morning he saw, in his mind, a picture of a prison cell, open on each side, with light running through it. He knew what it meant. He had to go home, face inevitable imprisonment; and walk the Christian way.

Fred Lemon, author of *Breakout*, described an even more vivid experience. He was doing time in Dartmoor, after taking part in a particularly brutal burglary which had left a jeweller within inches of death. If he had died, Lemon would have been hanged. As it was, he faced a long sentence in Britain's grimmest prison. One night, he awoke to find his prison cell flooded with light. He, too, saw the risen Lord. His life was transformed. His fellow-prisoners thought he was mad, but the vision remained his guiding force. When eventually he was released, he started to preach all over the country – even to policemen!

The presence of Christ does not have to be visible to be experienced. In *Death of a Guru*, Rabi Maharaj describes how he was chanting a prayer to the Hindu God of destruction, Shiva. He was standing on the edge of a cliff admiring the view beneath. Suddenly he heard an ominous rustling in the bushes. A huge snake came directly towards him. He felt hypnotized, unable to move. Although it lacked the cobra's hood, it reminded him of the huge snake Shiva wore around his neck. Now, despite his invocations, he wasn't going to escape, with this snake in front and a precipice behind. Close enough now for him to touch it, the snake raised its head. In that moment of terror, he remembered his mother's words: 'Rabi, if you're in real danger and nothing else seems to work, there's another God you can pray to. His name is Jesus.' 'Jesus! Help me!' he tried to yell. But the desperate cry was choked and hardly audible. To his utter astonishment, the snake dropped its head, and wriggled off rapidly into the undergrowth. Not long afterwards, although he was training to be a guru as his father had been, he was converted to Christianity.

A friend of mine suffered from appalling depression when pregnant with her first baby. Some time afterwards, still very shaken, she became a Christian. For a long time, faith was a struggle. Christianity gave her great strength, but doubts and depression still came. She had a very powerful intellect, and was sceptical of other people's 'experiences'. Like Thomas she seemed to miss out, though she continued faithfully to believe and to practise her faith. She seemed to have a fatalistic streak which meant that she didn't expect things to go right for her, though in other ways, and towards other people, she was full of life and hope. Then one day she was praying at the start of a Church service. Another depression seemed on its way. She saw no vision, heard no heavenly voice but just received an absolute conviction of the presence and loving care of God. Shortly afterwards she felt able to contemplate having another baby. The child was born safely, and despite severe physical illness, the mother has kept free from depression. God had become wonderfully real to her.

As Cowper puts it in a hymn,

Sometimes a light surprises the Christian as he sings;
It is the Lord who rises, with healing on his wings.

At this point, someone may be asking furiously, 'Why hasn't this happened to me?' 'How can I believe?' Here, we must take seriously Jesus' final words to Thomas: 'Because you have seen me, you believed; blessed are those who have not seen and yet have believed.' [NIV] We cannot manufacture deep spiritual experiences. They are given to some and not to others. The Apostle John might well have wondered why his brother James was executed by Herod (Acts 12.2), while Peter had a miraculous escape. Paul must have marvelled why he was granted a vision of the risen Lord, while most of the Jewish nation remained locked in darkness and unbelief (see Rom. 9). On the other hand, many experienced miracles of healing through Paul's prayers, while he had to suffer some painful physical condition (2 Cor. 12.7–10).

It is good that in recent years we have become more expectant. Time was when new converts would be told not to expect to feel anything. More recently the testimony of the Church has been full of accounts of guidance, healing and deliverance as well as suffering, doubt and death. It is right to teach people to expect some experience of God in their lives, though we shouldn't attempt to predict what form it will take.

For Thomas, the encounter with the risen Lord was necessary and decisive. In our time it has been fashionable to reject all of this. Forty years ago, Frank Morison, a journalist, set out to write an investigative critique of the resurrection. He expected to come to a sceptical conclusion. The book he wrote, entitled *Who Moved the Stone?*, turned out rather differently – it is one of the most precise and eloquent text books on the truth of the Resurrection that has ever been written.

What then is the evidence?[1] It comes from individuals, from their writings, and from history. We may know nothing more about Thomas, but we do know about some of the other apostles. We have already mentioned (Ch. 1) the change in Peter. It is difficult to imagine someone of Peter's fervent personality spending thirty years preaching about the resurrection without being utterly convinced of its truth. Could the man who lied when challenged by a serving girl have stood up to the whole Sanhedrin (Acts 4.19–21) unless he was utterly certain of the starting point of his message?

The change in James, the Lord's brother, is even more remarkable. In Jesus' lifetime, his family were sceptical. On one occasion (Mark 3.21,31), they wanted to seize him, presumably to lock him away – people were saying he was mad, even demon-possessed, and it was all very embarrassing. Elsewhere (John 7.5) John records that Jesus' brothers didn't believe in him. Each of the other evangelists records the failure of his ministry in his home town of Nazareth 'because of unbelief' (Matt. 13.55–8). Both Matthew and Mark seem to associate his family with this unbelief, and hence with the failure of his mission.

There is no evidence of any change of heart during Jesus' lifetime. Mary, his mother, of course remained a faithful member of the apostolic band, but nothing more is heard of James, or any of the other brothers, until the first pages of the Acts. Here (Acts 1.14) it is recorded that immediately after the ascension, the small band of believers gathered for prayer, 'All these [that is the disciples] with one accord devoted themselves to prayer, together with the women and Mary the mother of Jesus, *and with his brothers*.'

Soon afterwards (Acts 12.17; 15.13) James appears amongst the leaders of the apostolic Church. Paul acknowledges him to be one of the 'reputed pillars of the church' (Gal. 2.9). Later James was to suffer martyrdom. Josephus (*Antiquities* 9.1) records his death by stoning in AD 61. What had changed him from a sceptic into one who was 'faithful unto death'? Paul gives us the evidence:

> For I delivered to you as of first importance what I also received, that Christ died for our sins in accordance with the scriptures, that he was buried, that he was raised on the third day in accordance with the scriptures, and that he appeared to Cephas, then to the twelve. Then he appeared to more than five hundred brethen at one time, most of whom are still alive, though some have fallen asleep. Then he appeared to James, then to all the apostles. Last of all, as to one untimely born, he appeared also to me. For I am the least of the apostles, unfit to be called an apostle, because I persecuted the church of God (1 Cor. 15.3–9).

Then he appeared to James? What other explanation could account for the dramatic change? Why else would James have suffered dishonour and death on behalf of a brother whom he had avoided following while he lived?

The same sort of reasoning applies to Paul himself. Luke

regarded Paul's experience of the risen Christ as so remarkable that he writes of it three times in the few pages of the Acts (Acts 9.1–22; 22.6–21; 26.12–23). Paul's own writings are full of direct or indirect references to this experience. It was the basis of his apostleship, the basis of his hope, and the basis of his preaching. Rightly, Paul wrote: 'If Christ has not been raised, your faith is futile and you are still in your sins. Then those also who have fallen asleep in Christ have perished. If for this life only we have hoped in Christ, we are of all men to be pitied' (1 Cor. 15.17–19).

Paul writes too of 'receiving' the evidence of Christ's resurrection (1 Cor. 15.3 quoted above). His conversion occurred within a few years of the crucifixion (F.F. Bruce in his Commentary on Acts dates it tentatively in AD 33); but he writes of the resurrection evidence as received tradition. This was no late fable added to gild some icing upon hard Christian preaching; this was the basis of the faith from the beginning. Paul would have found it remarkable that in our own time the writers of *The Myth of God Incarnate* could have got so excited about Peter's description of Jesus as 'a man, attested to you by God' (Acts 2.22) as evidence that Jesus was in reality nothing more than a remarkable man, and yet in the same book totally discount Peter's next statement, 'But God raised him up!'

1 Corinthians 15 was written by AD 54. So the Resurrection evidence was first written down only twenty years or so after the event. Such a short time gap is almost unparalleled in ancient history. There is of course much other evidence which is generally cited: the empty tomb, the Gospels, the archaeological evidence of the markings on very early Christian graves, perhaps the Turin Shroud . . .

But the other fact which stands out is the very existence and survival of the Church. The story the first Christians were telling was not exactly calculated to appeal to any known audience. To the Jews, the scandal of crucifixion (pronounced an accursed death in Deuteronomy 21.23), quite apart from the blasphemy of apparently worshipping more than one God, was sufficient for them to dismiss Christianity as dangerous nonsense. To the Greeks, the whole story of resurrection was fairly amusing (Acts 17.32), reminding them of some of the sillier myths about their own gods whom they were ceasing to believe in. To those involved in the mystery cults, the lack of 'inner knowledge', the lack of exciting initiation ceremonies, and the distressing basis of alleged history, made this new religion seem a dull option compared with their exotic ways.

Yet, despite all this, and despite severe persecution at many times in the first centuries, the Church survived, and indeed flourished. Principally, because of the Easter faith! This sustained the martyrs, attracted the inquirer, gave faith to the preacher. It was the basis of all their preaching. 'If you confess with your lips that Jesus Christ is Lord and believe in your heart that God raised him from the dead, you will be saved' (Rom. 10.9). And the response to such preaching was often repentance, faith and discipleship (Acts 2.37 for instance).

But what of those who, like Thomas, find it easier to question than to believe? How can the honest agnostic find faith? How can an atheist meet God?

He may be gently challenged to examine his own integrity. Laurie, the narrator in Rose Macaulay's amusing and penetrating novel *The Towers of Trebizond*, responds to Father Chantry-Pigg's attempts to evangelize her with an uneasy silence. After he left her, she thought over her earlier life. Brought up an Anglican, she had lost her first faith.

> I was an agnostic through school and university, then, at twenty-three, took up with the Church again; but the Church met its Waterloo a few years later when I took up with adultery . . . and this adultery lasted on and on, and I was still in it now, steaming down the Black Sea to Trebizond, and I saw no prospect of its ending except with death – the death of one of three people . . .

Adultery did not stop her being fascinated by religion, but it did prevent any sort of commitment. The book has a poignant ending. Her lover is killed, and now her guilt is so great she cannot even bear to think of God, it hurts too much . . .

I spent a lot of time arguing with a group of senior boys at the school where I taught. They came very close to faith. But there seemed to be a block . . . These blocks are very common. They are the basis of Paul's great preliminary chapter in Romans 1. As he sets out to show that 'all have sinned and fall short of the glory of God' he sees the immorality of the age as one great sin that they have 'exchanged the truth about God for a lie and worshipped and served the creature rather than the Creator.' (Rom. 1.25)

For most of my school boys the block was, I think, a strong homosexual relationship with younger boys. A very different sort of block is that of the intellectual who lives in a logically closed shell. Not unlike his opposite, the rigid fundamentalist, he is unmoved by any argument. Arguments from experience prove nothing, arguments from history are indecisive, talk of resurrection is inconclusive; even 'God' is probably a logical impossibility. There seems no way through such a wall!

But salvation is by grace and not by argument. C.S. Lewis had argued himself into a pretty convinced atheism – an atheism which was shaken by discovering that many of those whom he most admired were Christians, or at least theists. Gradually his defences were demolished; miserably he acknowledged belief in God. Joy came only as he quickly moved on from belief in God to belief in Christ. His book *Surprised by Joy* is a marvellous account of his most gradual conversion.

Anthony Bloom's atheism was broken more simply, as he recounts in the Introduction to his *School for Prayer*. Challenged to go away and read the Gospels, he was struck by the simple directness of Mark's account. Suddenly, he sensed the actual presence of the Lord in the room with him, and another unbeliever was checkmated.

Sometimes, as I have suggested, the block is a moral one. Paul discovered this when he preached to Felix, the Roman governor in whose custody he lay. Felix came freely to hear Paul, but when Paul spoke of justice, self-control, and future judgement (Acts 24.25), Felix grew alarmed and said, 'Go away for the present; when I have an opportunity I will summon you'. Luke adds the interesting comment that he hoped Paul would give him some money. Little wonder he didn't like hearing about justice and self-control! Although he frequently went back to listen to Paul, there is no evidence that he was ever converted.

We have all met people like Felix, who try to escape from a serious challenge to faith by turning it into a topic of conversation. I remember a wealthy newspaper editor who visited our theological college. He claimed to be impressed by the social work done by the college. But as for himself, he had a yacht, a family, an interesting job. He was prepared to talk about religion, but, like Felix, he wasn't very interested in commitment. Once, leading a mission in a village, I was invited to meet the aged squire. He delighted himself by teasing me with stories about previous vicars who had admitted unbelief but had said 'it was good for the people to believe!' He wasn't remotely interested in commitment himself.

For many people, it is the humiliation of being seen to change that is too great. The thought of the neighbours ('Cor, you started going to church?') or friends ('You haven't joined the God Squad?') is often too much. That is one of the reasons why so many people don't get involved until there is a crisis or a break in their established pattern of life. (Moving house is a good time for initiating change, and any church which doesn't visit newcomers to its area is missing a golden opportunity.)

But still the intellectual gap remains. We cannot 'prove' our faith. So how can the honest agnostic – the man who has no apparent moral or intellectual barriers and who is willing to act if convinced – be persuaded to believe?

He may try the idea of assuming for a while that Christianity is true, trying to look at things from a Christian perspective and to imagine what it is like to believe. He may then discover that life makes a great deal more sense, and has potentially far deeper meaning, than he has realized before. Then perhaps he will be readier to respond in faith. It is like asking someone wavering about marriage, to imagine and to try and experience what marriage is really like, to get beyond the ceremony, into the actual experience.

The wedding analogy is a good one. We do not know what our bride is really like, and she doesn't know what we are really like. We exchange promises, we seal the covenant with a ring, and then we set out on the great adventure together. So it is with faith! God has given us his promises, we give ours as best we can, and his seal is the gift of the Holy Spirit.

Another person might be prepared to commit himself to go regularly either to church or to an inquirer's group. The worship of the one, and the intellectual stimulus of the other, frequently lead the genuine seeker right through to faith.

In the end, there are many roads to faith. Like the ways into the L-shaped field, some involve struggles and false turnings, some are relatively simple and straightforward. The magnet, Christ, stands at the centre of the field drawing all men unto himself (John 12.32). There, perhaps, is the best analogy of all. How often do we ask ourselves as Jesus did his friends, 'What manner of man is this? Whom do I think he is?'

When faith finally is given there will be a necessary response.

This poem indicates both the response and the gateway to spiritual power.

> My hands were filled with many things
> That I did precious hold
> As any treasure of a King's –
> Silver, or gems, or gold
> The Master came and touched my hands
> (The scars were in his own)
> And at his feet my treasures sweet
> Fell shattered, one by one
> 'I must have empty hands' said He
> 'Wherewith to work My works through thee'.
>
> My hands were stained with marks of toil,
> Defiled with dust of earth;
> And I my work did oft time soil,
> And render little worth.
> The Master came and touched my hands
> (And crimson were his own)
> But when amazed, I gazed
> Lo! every stain was gone
> 'I must have cleansed hands' said He
> 'Wherewith to work My works through thee'.
>
> My hands were growing feverish
> And cumbered with much care!
> Trembling with haste and eagerness
> Nor folded oft in prayer.
> The Master came and touched my hands
> (With healing in his own)
> And calm and still to do His will
> They grew – the fever gone.
> 'I must have quiet hands' said He
> 'Wherewith to work My works for Me'.
>
> My hands were strong in fancied strength,
> But not in power divine,
> And bold to take up tasks at length,
> That were not His but mine,
> The Master came and touched my hands
> (And might was in his own)
> But mine since then have powerless been
> Save his are laid thereon

'And it is only thus' said He
'That I can work My works through thee'.[2]

NOTE

1   For detailed argument on the evidence for the Resurrection, see
    I Believe in the Resurrection of Jesus by G.E. Ladd (Hodder &
    Stoughton 1979) and *The Day Death Died* by Michael Green (IVP
    1982).
2   Quoted in *Quiet Talks on Power* by S.D. Gordon (Revell 1960).

5 *Wholeness*

A few years ago I was involved in arranging the first healing conference in our diocese. It was not a great success. The first speaker, misjudging the meeting, decided that we were all raving Pentecostalists who believed that God would heal anything and everything if only we had enough faith. Consequently, though he spoke movingly about his work as a hospital chaplain, his attitude towards the healing ministry was negative. As far as he was concerned, faith and prayer made very little difference to the terminally ill – they died. He also implied that there was little healing in the apostolic Church – citing Acts.

In group discussion, I challenged this view. 'What about Paul in Malta?' 'Ah', he replied. 'After the healing of the islanders, Luke the doctor says "and they brought *us* gifts" (Acts 28.10). This was in gratitude for his herbal remedies which had cured them!' When I replied that these medicines would surely have been lost in the storm at sea, he looked displeased and it became clear that no dialogue was going to be possible between us.

The whole question of healing does raise very difficult questions. What is God's will? Has the Church still got a genuine healing ministry? How does it relate to a person's whole salvation? And why is there so much suffering?

It was this last question which troubled the disciples when they asked Jesus concerning a blind man: 'Rabbi, who sinned, this man or his parents, that he was born blind?' (John 9.2). They had seen Jesus heal many different people. They themselves had been sent out on occasions to heal the sick, and now they wanted to know the answer to an important question. Why was this man blind? (And that man paralyzed, and that woman bent double, and that little girl dying . . .?)

On this occasion, Jesus emphatically declared that no one had sinned. This man's blindness was going to be the gateway for God's glory to be seen in his life. But even the disciples must have realized that Jesus wasn't pronouncing a new formula to fit all cases of unexplained illness.

Elsewhere we find Jesus hinting at, or openly declaring, different causes for sickness. The paralytic man (Mark 2.1–12) needed his sins forgiven before he received his healing. The woman with a bent back (Luke 13.10–17) had a 'spirit of infirmity'. Jesus described her as a daughter of Abraham whom Satan had bound for eighteen years. She was healed with a few brief authoritative words. Jesus also seems to have discerned the direct hand of Satan in the illness of the leper (Mark 1.40–5). The oldest textual reading says that he was moved with indignation (as opposed to pity) – presumably at the ravages of Satan on the man's body. Sometimes, as with Peter's mother-in-law (Luke 4.38–9), Jesus addressed the disease and commanded it to leave. On one occasion (John 5.2–15), he asked a man a seemingly strange question: 'Do you want to be healed?' The implication was that the man might have grown so accustomed to illness that life would be simpler for him if he wasn't healed and had to continue to depend on others.

So we can discern at least four strands of illness. It may, of course, have straightforward physical causes. Or it may be caused by sin, selfishness or Satan – or any combination of these!

To return to the blind man. Jesus apparently had no conversation with him. He immediately went up to him, anointed his eyes with a paste made of spittle and earth, and told him to go and wash in the pool of Siloam. Unlike Naaman (2 Kings 5) the man didn't object; he went straight to the pool, and received his sight. Then his troubles began! Some doubted that he was the same man, others questioned him about his healing and tried to destroy his confidence by asserting that the healing was not from God – God would never heal on the Sabbath! Even his parents declined to support him. The religious leaders refused to accept his testimony and threw him out of the synagogue. It was at that moment that Jesus again came alongside him. Gently he asked him, 'Do you believe in the Son of Man?' and then revealed, 'It is he who speaks to you.' The man declared his faith and worshipped Jesus.

Here, as on many other occasions, Jesus showed that he was concerned with more that just the man's physical condition. That was why he drew into the open the woman with the issue of blood (Mark 5.24–34, and Chapter 1 here). She needed to be seen to be healed, she needed to be spiritually whole as well as physically clean. That was why he was distressed with the nine lepers (Luke 17.17). They had missed much of the blessing intended for them!

This is a major hazard in the healing ministry. At one of the first such meetings I attended, the 'healer' preached a very long sermon based on Isaiah 53. Rightly he stressed the connection between the cross, healing and salvation. The room was small and crowded, and people were getting very restless. 'Why doesn't he get on with the healing bit?' someone muttered. When he did eventually get on with the healing part, the results were amazing. He discerned that someone had a breathing problem and a woman with a terrible condition was healed instantly. A woman with severely ulcerated legs took off her bandages and found that they were completely cured. But despite these and other physical miracles, there was no real spiritual change and those who were healed seemed to go on as normal.

Don Double, leader of the Good News Crusade, once told me that he found less real fruit from the evangelism on their healing night than on others. He feels that people make a 'decision' because they think it will improve their prospects of physical healing. The evangelist Fred Smith, who has a remarkable public ministry in Oxford, experiences the same problem. Many come forward at his meetings confessing Jesus as Lord, but relatively few begin any sort of realistic discipleship.

I shall never forget the first person for whose physical healing I prayed. My mother-in-law had had a word from the Lord that a lady who was to visit us that day would be healed of a back condition. I fervently hoped that we wouldn't be called on to pray. All this sort of thing was very new to me. But at the end of the day, our visitor suddenly complained about her back.

'Mummy, your back's a bore!' her ten-year-old daughter said, whereupon her mother withdrew in tears to the kitchen.

I followed her, and rather reluctantly I said, 'I think my mother-in-law has a gift of healing; would you like us to pray?' To my horror she agreed! As soon as we started to pray she was healed. To prove it, she jumped up and down. Naively, I expected her and her family to become Christians then and there. But none of those present did, although they were appreciative and moved. Later, her husband, a doctor, persuaded her that her back had been getting better anyway.

The main beneficiary from this incident was me! Quite apart from learning to value my mother-in-law's spiritual judgement, I stepped out with some faith into a new ministry of praying for the sick!

The next healing situation that I was involved with had various connections with the man at the Pool of Bethesda (John 5). When our first child, Rachel, was born we prayed that her birth might help us to get to know our neighbours. A few days later, a woman did start talking to Rachel and then to us. She turned out to have a very painful hand condition which none of the hospital professors could help. Her mother had had German measles when pregnant and this illness had caused the hand deformity which plagued her. She was very depressed, and had plenty of family troubles as well as the physical pain. Soon after we met her she became a Christian. I started to pray for her hand. She testified to an improvement, and then I got a surprise. As I held her hand, pain shot into my hand. It was so intense that I could pray for only a few minutes. For the next few weeks, I used to visit her every evening. Gradually her hand got so much better that she was able to take a job as a taxi driver!

She moved away, but we still kept in touch. Five years ago she got another shock. She was diagnosed with cancer of the liver, stomach, and colon, and told that she had three months to live. Many people went to see her, usually in small groups, to pray. To begin with, there was little progress – just survival. She lived, against expectation, to Christmas. She was being treated with some new drug, but I don't think the doctors had any real hope of a cure. After Christmas, things changed. Sometimes, when people prayed, she felt a fire in her stomach. X-rays confirmed that the cancer was diminishing. All along she had said she wanted to be healed – but couldn't cope unless it was gradual!

Just before Easter, as we were talking together, I felt that I should read John 5 – the story of the man at the pool of Bethesda. I asked her how old she was. Thirty seven! 'So you have been ill for thirty eight years!' She looked puzzled, and then it clicked. She had been ill since her mother had had German measles. I told her that I felt confident that this was a word from God that she would get better. A few weeks later, after another prayer session, she again felt the burning sensation in her stomach. It lasted for a whole week. At the end of it, more X-rays showed that virtually all trace of the disease had gone. To the amazement of the doctors she is alive and well today.

I have prayed with a number of other young people who

were terminally ill, who did not recover, and in every case there was a great sense of God's grace. A number of them seemed to be converted during their illness, and all died relatively peacefully believing in Christ as Lord and Saviour.

One of these was a young schoolmaster. He lived in the north of England, and came occasionally to Oxford for medical treatment. He had a progressive illness which was slowly destroying his mobility. We became great friends, and would talk, and pray, each time that he came south. He became a regular communicant at his local parish church, and definitely moved into real faith as his life ebbed away. After he died, I became friends with one of his colleagues, Peter, who had a schoolmaster fellowship at Oxford. He took me out to dinner. After dinner, we relaxed and sat in his room sipping port, when suddenly a whole host of unexpected troubles surfaced. 'Apart from anything else,' he said, 'I've terrible migraines which attack me at about five o'clock nearly every morning.' I picked up the Bible that lay on the table beside the port. Something within me said 'Habbakuk 3.4'. 'His brightness was like the light, rays flashed from his hand . . .' It wasn't exactly in context, but it sounded like an accurate description of a migraine. Peter confirmed that he could not endure any intensity of light during an attack. We prayed together for the migraines and the other matters which troubled him. He hasn't had a migraine since, and everything else that we prayed about has greatly improved.

In the case of the woman with the bent back (Luke 13.10–17), Luke states that she had a 'spirit of infirmity'. Jesus said that she had been bound by Satan for eighteen years. How much illness can we attribute to the direct attack of Satan?

Clearly this is a difficult question (and very much related to the topics discussed in the next chapter) but I have known a number of instances where this seemed to be the case.

A long time ago, an ex-missionary told me that her aunt, who was a spiritualist, was trying to transmit her powers to her. She was suffering from a painful and embarrassing rash, which she attributed to having worn clothes given her by the aunt. I must confess that I was very sceptical. But I promised that we would pray that if in any direct way Satan, or his servant her aunt, were responsible, she would be healed. The rash cleared up amazingly fast; her doctor was amazed and delighted.

More recently a girl came to see me suffering quite badly from anorexia nervosa. It had started some years earlier when her grandmother, of whom she was very fond, had died. So far, it was a classical medical diagnosis. But there was a strange twist. Her grandmother's mother had been a spiritualist. Grandmother, while not a spiritualist, had seen no harm in 'contacting' mother. A chain of spiritual disobedience had been set up in the family (see the clear warning in Exodus 20.5). When we very gently prayed for this to be broken, the girl was set free!

Dr Kenneth McAll, whose work amongst the depressed has been highlighted in some of the national newspapers, and recently in his book, *Healing the Family Tree*, helped me to see that this line of spiritual disobedience was a serious cause of bondage in many families. While not condemning our ancestors, none of us need to inherit troubles due to their dabblings in forbidden pastimes. We have troubles enough of our own!

Depression is one of the commonest of the enemy's weapons amongst believers and non-believers. It is one of the most appalling experiences. Those of us who are liable to it need to be able to read the warning signs and, as an act of will, seek prayer at its onset. Prayer is a very powerful counter-weapon, although usually the last thing in the world that the depressed person wants is to be prayed with! A friend who suffered from acute depression eventually confessed to a sin that she had committed in a previous job. We prayed and the power of the depression was broken. It only returned really seriously when she strayed along a dangerous path, and disappeared when again she confessed, and sought prayer.

Jesus must frequently have been exhausted by the long periods of ministry to the sick. This exhaustion can lead us not to want to pray for people. It is precisely at such times that those of us called to this work must keep going.

I belonged to a small house group where at one time everyone seemed ill and out of sorts. After a rather routine house communion, we prayed for one another. Chris (the father converted at his baby's baptism mentioned in Chapter 1) asked us to pray for the baby, now about a year old, who had been very sick for a long time. An old lady reluctantly allowed us to pray for her stiff neck. She didn't tell us that she was having trouble with her eyes, but we prayed generally for her health. The next day, I was writing in my occasional prayer diary, 'Lord, if you're serious about the healing ministry please let there be some clear result from last night' when the phone rang. It was Chris's wife ringing up to say that the baby was completely better. Nor was that the end of it. A few weeks later the old lady had her eyes tested before an operation. They were completely well! Some time after that Chris's back seized up. He came for prayer and to his surprise was able to go back to work immediately. Even more amazing was the illness of his own father who was diagnosed to have terminal cancer. He appeared to enter his final illness, the family prayed, he suddenly recovered and the next X-rays were clear. The family doctor was astounded.

But it would be very misleading to write as though the healing ministry today is one long success story. We have had many puzzles, many disappointments, but few disasters. In nearly every case, people seem to grow spiritually, or get better physically, or both, as a result of a prayer. Often the results are partial. This puzzles some people. They feel that since Jesus' healing ministry was always completely effective, so should that of his Church be.

I believe 1 Corinthians 13 provides a key. 'Our knowledge is imperfect, our prophecy is imperfect' and surely too 'our healing is imperfect'. We thank God for the signs of his grace that we do see. Obviously we try to discover why people are not healed.

This brings us to the question of faith. Often people who are not healed, especially at big public meetings, are left feeling guilty about their lack of faith.

Jesus commended faith in the context of healing, but seems never to have insisted on it. The friends of the paralytic man (Mark 2) obviously exercised a certain amount of faith on his behalf, but there is no evidence that the man himself had any faith. The blind man (John 9) whose case we have already discussed had no opportunity to display any faith – all that was needed was obedience!

The two examples of faith most commended by Jesus were both in non-Jewish circles. The Canaanite woman (Matt. 15.21–8) cried out to Jesus, and at first received no reply. Undaunted she persisted and, when faced with an apparent refusal, argued her case with skill and tact. Jesus commended her faith and her daughter was healed.

The centurion (Luke 7.1–10) was even more confident. He

did not feel worthy to ask Jesus to come into his house to see his slave. Instead he sent a message to Jesus, just asking him to say the word and his servant would be healed. This simple faith greatly appealed to Jesus and the servant was healed instantly.

There are not many other examples of absent healing in the Gospels; usually Jesus was in physical contact with the person. Absent healing still occurs today, but it requires considerable faith in those who are praying.

Fred Smith, whom I mentioned earlier, has told me a number of stories from his own congregation. One of the loveliest concerned a woman who prayed for her deaf nephew. When she got home from the service, she was greeted by an astonished phone call from her sister – the nephew had just come downstairs saying that he could hear!

On certain occasions, we do seem to receive a special gift of faith (see 1 Cor. 12.9) for a particular situation. I remember going to an intensive care unit with my then rector, Michael Green, to pray for a girl who was unconscious after a cycling accident. After we had prayed for her, Michael got up from his knees and calmly informed her anxious parents that she would get better. At that time she was only given a 50–50 chance of survival by the doctors. In fact, she recovered more quickly than the doctors deemed likely. Her parents, who were not Christians, were unimpressed. They presumed that Michael said that sort of thing to all waiting relatives!

A year later, we were called to the same unit to pray for a girl who had been brutally attacked by a madman in a shop. She, too, was a member of our church. This time neither of us had any sense that it was right to pray for healing. We commended her to God, and very soon afterwards she died.

Prayer with the dying is a very special privilege. A neighbour of ours had a second primary cancer. As he was a faithful member of another church, I wasn't primarily involved in ministering to him, but one evening, Fred Smith had come to our home for a cup of tea and prayer of thanksgiving – we had just finished a marathon evening of praying for the sick at St Aldate's – and we met my neighbour's wife on the doorstep. It seemed like a God-given coincidence, and I asked if we could pray with her husband. He was delighted and testified afterwards to an amazing sense of light and peace. Ten days later we had a deep conversation about the future life which I found immensely stimulating and encouraging; two days after that he died peace-fully – months sooner than expected. A long wearisome illness had been cut short. His wife could only rejoice.

On another occasion I got involved in praying with a woman with a very serious cancer. She had been treated with platinum, and was clearly extremely ill. After an hour's talk, two of us anointed her with oil and prayed for her. She felt dramatically better and her next set of X-rays startled the doctors. For about six months she improved remarkably and then the illness regained the upper hand. Because she lived a long way away, I was only able to see her once more. She had grown much in faith. A few months later she died, but her local vicar reckoned that the last year had been a very important, a very special time for her and the family.

In each of these situations, though the person died, there was a sense of God's wholeness coming into a situation – the full-ness of salvation, holiness, wholeness, which seemed to trans-cend the actual physical illness and death.

There are few specific instructions about healing in the New Testament. It was certainly part of the apostolic training pro-gramme (see Luke 10.1–25; Mark 6.7–13; etc.). It was also cer-tainly part of the experience of the early Church. The classic teaching passage is James 5.13–18, which encourages all who are sick to seek anointing with oil by the elders of the Church. Francis McNutt in his book *Healing*[1] describes how this text became misused in the Catholic Church. Because the Latin has only one verb, *salvo*, which has the meaning both of physical and spiritual healing, the emphasis of the passage changed in the Vulgate from physical healing to salvation. Consequently anointing with oil, intended as a sacrament for healing, became the sacramental unction to the dying.

Anointing is now practised widely in many churches. It is a moving, and simple, service which we perform in obedience to Scripture. There is nothing magical about the oil (though sev-eral times I've known it seem to burn people who have been involved in occult practices). The burden of faith is on those who pray, the ministers, and not the patient, being pointed to the faith of Elijah! There is a helpful provision in James 5 for mutual confession of sin – sometimes those who are to do the praying need this just as much. Anointing with oil also acts as a focus to work towards. The sick man understands that something definite is going to be done, and has time to prepare himself for the occasion.

What is the place of the healing ministry within the whole plan of salvation?

Jesus healed all sorts of people. Certainly he sought to minister to both their physical and their spiritual needs, but often the people concerned must have missed the connection. Nine of the ten lepers did so, and the crowds who were looking for signs and wonders showed no obvious signs of penitence and faith.

In Jesus' lifetime, healing was an authentic sign of the coming of the Kingdom. When John the Baptist inquired, plaintively, from prison, 'Are you he who is to come or shall we look for another?' (Matt. 11.3) Jesus answered: 'Go and tell John what you hear and see: the blind receive their sight and the lame walk, lepers are cleansed and the deaf hear, and the dead are raised up, and the poor have the good news preached to them . . .'

The healing miracles were a necessary part of the Messianic mission. They were subordinate to the preaching of the good news (see especially Mark 1.38, but they were important signs of God's gracious favour to the people).

It is difficult to be certain how important healing was in the apostolic Church. Dramatic miracles are recounted in the book of Acts (the man at the Gate Beautiful, ch. 3; Aeneas and Dorcas, 9.32–40; Eutychus, 20.7–12); there were periods of intense healing activity (Peter, 5.12–16; Stephen, 6.8; Philip, 8.4–8; Paul, 19.11–12 and 28.7–10); and other long periods when little or no healing is recorded. Certainly the healing miracles helped Philip's evangelism, when 'the multitudes with one accord gave heed to what was said by Philip, when they heard him and saw the signs which he did' (8.6). Luke also records, after Paul's healing and deliverance ministry in Ephesus, 'So the word of the Lord grew and prevailed mightily' (19.20). Tradition, too, traces the conversion of Malta to Christianity right back to Paul's visit. Here again, as we saw earlier, the healing ministry seems to have opened the hearts of the people. The healing ministry in Malta left a sweet fragrance behind, which must have assisted the growth of the gospel.

Sometimes the signs and wonders harden opposition. The High Priests were filled with jealousy because Peter healed the people (5.17); Stephen's ministry of signs and wonders provoked the opposition which led to his martyrdom (6.8ff.). Just recently, I received a letter telling of healing and conversions at a mission hospital in a Muslim country. The police couldn't protect one of the converts from her angry family, and the hospital had to be closed.

I believe that the healing ministry is again becoming an important part of God's saving activity. In our weary and sick society, people are longing for good news. Despite the advances of modern science and the skills of modern medicine, people are looking more than ever for signs of the supernatural. The healing ministry also cuts across all barriers of churchmanship. Roman Catholics, Anglicans, Free Churchmen, House Church people, can gather together to lay hands on the sick. They have the same faith, even if the manner of prayer may be different. The healing touch revitalizes dying faith.

A story is told of a healing service in an overseas cathedral. The leader hauled the bishop in with the command 'Come and lay hands on the sick – that's what bishops are for!' The bishop obeyed! To his surprise, the lame threw their crutches away and others were healed. His ministry and pastoral vision were transformed. Isn't this just what we should expect our bishops to be doing?

NOTE

1 Francis McNutt has written a number of books on healing. I would recommend these as basic reading on the subject.

6 *Freedom*

'Go home to your friends and tell them how much the Lord has done for you, and how he has had mercy upon you' (Mark 5.19).

Jesus and his disciples had crossed the Lake of Galilee. It had been an awesome voyage for the disciples. They had been terrified of the fierce storm, and amazed by the way Jesus had calmed it. Soon they received another demonstration of his authority. They had hardly got out of the boat, when an extra-ordinary man raced up towards them. Possibly he was dragging pieces of the chains which had been used in a futile attempt to subdue him. Probably his body was lacerated with self-inflicted wounds. Certainly he was shrieking and gesticulating wildly.

This man was as much a social outcast as a leper was. The villagers could see no hope for him, and had tried to get rid of him by chaining him to the tombs in a desolate region. There he lived, crying out, cutting himself, and foraging for food in a wild, unfriendly area. He was immensely strong, yet utterly helpless. Within him dwelt some fearful force which sought to destroy him. Yet this force drove him relentlessly to meet Jesus. Just as a moth is attracted to a light that will destroy it, so the devil within the man drove him towards Jesus.

Possibly, at first, the demons within, recognizing an enemy, hoped to overpower Jesus by calling out his name – demonic powers in those days, as is still obvious in primitive animistic societies, try to gain control over their enemies by use of their name.[1] The man, or the spirits within him, was driven into a confrontation with Jesus. The disciples were doubtless amazed spectators as Jesus, quietly and firmly, addressed not the man, but the evil powers within him, and commanded the evil spirit to leave. For the only recorded time in Jesus' ministry there was a brief hesitation. The demons argued and sought to be left alone. Jesus addressed the man again, and asked him his name. The curious reply came, 'My name is Legion; for we are many'. The spirits had apparently taken over the man's vocal chords, and replied in a general way.[2] Then, recognizing Jesus' authority, and realizing the futility of their situation, they begged

Jesus not to send them away from the area. They obviously regarded it as a good hunting ground. Perhaps, as in the parable of the room swept clean (Matt. 12.45)[3] when seven worse spirits returned, they intended to return to the man once Jesus had left the area. They then made an even more specific request – they asked to enter a large herd of swine. Jesus agreed!

There were three dramatic consequences. The herd of pigs was destroyed. Their owners, and all the local people, were furious and afraid. The man was set free – 'clothed and in his right mind'. The destruction of the pigs, which has caused much perplexity, showed the murderous intention of the demonic forces. Their first aim was to destroy the man. If they couldn't achieve that, anything else would do – demonic forces are utterly destructive, and also seem to give people great strength. By allowing them to enter the pigs, Jesus showed the man that he was now completely free. Nothing else would have convinced him. The loss of a herd of pigs, illegally farmed in the Jewish–Greek region of Decapolis, was secondary. Jesus could have cast the demons straight into hell;[4] but he chose, for the sake of the man, to permit them to enter the pigs.

The men who herded the pigs disappeared with some haste. They must have been terrified, and probably feared being held responsible for this financial disaster. The townspeople, not perhaps too surprisingly, asked Jesus to leave, at once. The mighty works of God can be very disturbing; most of us faced with such power would want to hide. (This is why the ministry of deliverance, when needed today, is best carried out in private if possible.)

The man, for his part, would have gladly left the region, to follow Jesus and learn more from him. The whole area had unhappy memories for him, and the reaction of the townsfolk, who probably included members of his family, had been distinctly hostile. But Jesus gave him a far harder task. 'Go back to your family, and tell them how much the Lord has done for you.' The man had to go back, and bear witness to Jesus, in the very place that wanted to be rid of him! Amazingly, the man obeyed.

Amazingly, because the Gospels are full of incidents in which people, who have been healed or helped by Jesus, do the exact opposite of what he asks them to do (Mark 1.45 for example). But this man, who up to a few minutes before would have been incapable of performing the simplest rational action, now immediately did what Jesus asked. He went and told the people what had happened. 'And all the people were amazed.' [NIV]

Such things happen today. People are still gripped by these sorts of forces. People still display, amongst other characteristics, the extraordinary wildness and strength of the Gadarene man.

One evening, Jane and I were entertaining a 'Christian psychologist and her husband to dinner, and the discussion turned to these matters. While we were in the middle of it, the bell rang and a very distressed man stood at the door. I knew him well, although he'd never visited us. I spent some time trying to discover what was wrong. Eventually, in floods of tears, he confessed that he had attacked his wife. I hurried to see her, leaving those at the dinner party to look after him. She appeared remarkably resilient, and explained that he had a drink problem.

After about a quarter of an hour, I returned home to a somewhat disorganized house. The dining-room table was on its side, the guests were retreating in all directions, two policemen and a fellow clergyman were trying to restrain our visitor who was snarling like a wild animal and attempting to bite the table leg. Eventually I accompanied him to the police station. Both the clergyman and my wife shared with me their conviction that there was something demonic about his behaviour (and the psychologist didn't dissent!).

I made it clear that we would not prefer any charges. The police were sympathetic and helpful. They tried to calm the man down, and from time to time he would stop growling and become fairly normal. At other times, he displayed enough strength to make four officers distinctly wary. A doctor was called and she diagnosed that he had a 'binge drink' problem. Once, when he was calm, I casually asked if he had ever been involved in any occult practices. Immediately he started to blaspheme, and snarled out some of his experiences when in the services.

For his own safety, and that of his family, he spent the night in the cells. After consultation with the very helpful doctors (from my own practice!) it was agreed that he should first be treated for the alcohol problem. I shared the spiritual side and added 'If I'm right we'll have a repetition of this when he's stone cold sober.' The doctors smiled politely and we left it at that.

He progressed well. The drink problem disappeared, his family were happy together, and he started to come to church. But still he felt uneasy. Then one beautiful afternoon in May (about six months after the first incident), he came to talk to me. He was worried about a board with letters round it that he'd picked up and taken to his allotment, and he was sad that, although he came to church, he didn't really feel part of it. I explained that I felt he needed to renounce all connection with the occult past – and the present, as I deducted that the thing he had found was an ouija board – and that he should retake his baptismal vows, which would have the effect both of releasing the past and making a positive and clear profession of faith in the present.

While I was talking, he suddenly said 'You'd better pray quickly.' Before I could pray more than a few words, the very solid wooden chair on which he was sitting had split beneath him into three and he was sitting in a heap, shaking all over, on the floor. I was pretty terrified. My rector, with whom I had mainly worked in this field, was far away writing a book – ironically, *I Believe in Satan's Downfall*; and my other two colleagues were absent playing cricket for the diocese! Somewhat hesitantly, I told the man *in the name of the Lord* to stop shaking. Praise God, he did! We then drove to his allotment and collected the ouija board, which I burnt. I said a brief prayer and arranged a time for a small service for him to reaffirm his baptismal vows. In the meantime, I consulted our suffragan bishop who was very understanding, and my medical practice, who were surprised, but gave their agreement for the service to go ahead.

The service took place in church about five days later, with one of my colleagues and two lay leaders present. We had an anxious moment waiting for our friend to come. He told us afterwards that he had found it incredibly difficult to enter the church, but sensed that he must. I took the baptismal vows in reverse order and asked him first, 'Do you renounce evil?' specifying various things which he'd previously mentioned. For about thirty seconds he shook, then, quite clearly, he replied, 'I renounce evil'. At once he looked quite different. Peace flooded into his face, and his eyes sparkled. We proceeded with the other vows and anointed him with oil for wholeness (see Mark 6.13; Jas. 5.13–16; Isa. 61.3). He left the church rejoicing and the next day called at my home to testify

59

how different he felt. Since then he has been a faithful member of the congregation. He continues to testify to the difference that Christ makes and the reality of the evil from which he was set free.

This is just one of a number of examples from my own experience. It would be wrong to imagine that there will always be violence (as in the destruction of the pigs or the chair), but there is always a tremendous sense of release when the period of ministry is over. Both the person prayed for and the ministers experience a wonderful sense of elation and of the Lord's presence.

One early discovery which we made, as a team involved in this type of ministry, was of the power of Christian symbols: consecrated water, oil, the cross, and the holy communion. Michael Green, in *I Believe in Satan's Downfall*, describes an example of this.

> One person under the influence of multiple demon possession crowed at me, 'Ah, you haven't got any holy water.' 'I have,' I replied, and at once consecrated some water in a glass in the name of the Trinity, and proceeded to sprinkle her. The effect was immediate, electric and amazing. She jumped as if she had been scalded. The spirit manifested itself powerfully, and in due course departed.

We have seen people who have drunk consecrated water and have felt terribly sick or experienced choking, whereas when the ministry was completed they were able to drink freely from the same glass. Once someone touched some consecrated water and fell into a deep sleep. When she woke, about half an hour later, she was completely well and a long and difficult period of ministry was over.

In Mark 6.13 we read that the first disciples 'cast out many demons, and anointed with oil many that were sick and healed them' – thus making a connection between exorcism, healing and anointing. I believe it is beneficial, after a period of ministry, to anoint the person with oil. This quiet, gentle ministry gives a chance to pray for healing of any after-effects, to pray for an infilling with the Holy Spirit (and thus to avoid the unfortunate situation described in Matthew 12.43, where deliverance only makes a bad situation worse). If the previous ministry has been incomplete, anointing will induce any remaining problems to manifest themselves.

Michael Green also describes how he used the sign of the cross to protect himself when being attacked by someone with a knife who was under demonic influence. Frequently, demonized people will close their eyes tightly rather than look at even the smallest cross.

Holy Communion is, of course, the most powerful of all such symbols. People with a demonic problem are often quite unable to receive communion (and, of course, should not be encouraged to do so) until they have been set free. It is wise to hold a service of communion in a building which has been prayed through, and people who have been set free should take communion as soon as is practicable. I once ministered to a girl who had just taken a tentative step of commitment to Christ from a background of spiritualism and the Jehovah's Witnesses. She had been driven to spiritualism to 'contact' her dead fiancé, with whom she had had a suicide pact. After praying for her, we held a simple communion service and prayed for his influence on her to be broken. Afterwards, one of the team described seeing a man walk out of my study wearing an overcoat with a patch on it. 'That's him,' said the girl. 'I mended the patch.' I don't know what my colleague saw – whether it was a vision or a spirit – but it certainly helped the girl to believe that she was free.

Perhaps that is why Christian symbols are important – they 'help belief'. A free churchman, much involved in this ministry, once asked a bishop why he dressed up in a mitre, and used holy water, etc., on those occasions. The bishop replied: 'The symbols help the faith of those for whom we are praying.'

Occasionally the spirits speak through the afflicted person, using his vocal cords. Jesus usually forbade this (Luke 4.41), though interestingly enough not in the story with which this chapter begins. The first time I experienced this phenomenon was when a young woman stumped around my kitchen, talking and walking like an old man. Usually, however, the words used are a clue to the source of the problem. One woman was troubled with a Greek-sounding word. She couldn't stop thinking about it. She also brought me 500 paracetamol tablets which she had bought under the spirit's influence. I was not inclined to take the matter seriously until I tracked down the word in the Apocrypha. It was the name of a very unpleasant spirit who tried to persuade Tobit's wife to commit suicide.

Recently I was asked to visit the home of a man who was

critically ill – mainly because the family felt that the house had an oppressive, evil atmosphere. I am not sensitive to such things, but I took with me someone who is, and she confirmed it. I was just about to pray for the man, who seemed to have a rather vague, unformed faith, when I asked him about any connections he might have had with spiritualism.

'Oh, yes,' he said. 'We had a friend who came to pray for my healing. She went into a trance and turned into a German doctor!'

We prayed through the house. In one room, my prayer partner felt that further prayers were needed. When we went back downstairs to the room where the seance had taken place, I asked to see the chair on which the medium had sat. 'It's upstairs,' was the reply. It was in fact in the one room where the most prayer had seemed necessary – a small confirmation that we were doing something important. We finished praying through the house, prayed again for the man, and left.

I saw that man only once more. He and his wife were wonderfully cheerful, and the whole house felt quite different. A few days later he died, and his wife was greatly helped by the spiritual uplift of the last week. A colleague who knew nothing of this ministry remarked to me how amazingly changed the man was in the last few days of his life. It is deeply humbling to have some small part in such ministry.

I have been privileged to see a number of such transformations. The sense of relief when a person is set free, the usually delightful and faithful discipleship that follows, makes such ministry, although alarming and spiritually draining, wonderfully worth while. Small wonder that the seventy (Luke 10.17) returned with joy rejoicing that even the demons were subject to them in the name of Jesus.

It would be idle to deny that such ministry is controversial, and equally that it is open to considerable abuse. But to deny it to people who really need it, is to fail them at a point of deep need. It is understandable that many people question whether evil spirits exist. But this leads to a view of Jesus' ministry which either says that he was wrong in this very fundamental area, or explains it away by saying that he was using the thought categories of the day. Bishop Ryle, writing in the last century and with no actual experience of this ministry, observes in his commentary on the incident in Mark 5[5] that Africans living in equatorial forests might well doubt the existence of igloos. They would however be foolish to deny the possibility without first visiting the arctic. I freely admit that, before reluctantly getting involved in this ministry, I, too, would have been fairly sceptical.

The ministry of deliverance was common in apostolic times, and it continued in the succeeding centuries.[6] Christian baptism used to contain a form of exorcism. Many subsequent difficulties would be avoided if, in adult baptism and confirmation, the question 'Do you renounce evil?' was amplified to make it clear that this involved renouncing all past connection with ouija boards, tarot cards, white magic . . .

In many cases, a clear public renunciation (not unlike the celebrated bonfire in Acts 19.19) is quite sufficient to free the person from any ill effects. There is no evidence to suggest that everyone who has been involved in these things is demonized – just as not everyone catches measles in an epidemic. Nevertheless it is wise to make such a renunciation. Quite small levels of involvement can produce unfortunate and unexpected results.

A man who was involved in one of our leadership training courses shared with me that he was in bondage to a particular temptation. He didn't tell me what it was, only that its intensity alarmed him. When I asked him if he had had any past occult involvement, he looked surprised. Eventually, he related some minor incident as a teenager. After a while, he saw the need to renounce this, we prayed and he left. A few days later he was testifying, in public, to an amazing sense of peace, and complete confidence that the grip of the temptation had been broken.

Such ministry is often a good preparation for a time of praying for an infilling of the Spirit. Once when I was conducting a healing seminar at a renewal conference, a lay leader stopped me and admitted to feeling uncomfortable. I suggested that this might have several causes – he might find the whole subject troubling, I might have said something untrue or unwise, or he might be in some sort of bondage. I was at this time talking about the effect of the spiritual disobedience of previous generations (Exod. 20.5), and, in particular, was talking about freemasonry which, despite its Christian overtones, at the very least takes people through strange initiations and to generally deist, rather than specifically Christian, assertions. After the session, he remembered that his father had been a Mason. This led us next morning to a time of general ministry in which many more serious things were renounced, and many people felt a new freedom. One clergyman, in desperate trouble, now felt able to receive prayer and counselling with much more expectation of help than ever before. That evening, at a communion service, there was a tremendous sense of peace and God's blessing to all who were there. The lifting of the clouds in the morning was a necessary preliminary before the light and joy of the evening.

I believe that bondage is also caused, especially to those seeking to grow into effective discipleship, by involvement with Eastern religions and yoga[7] or TM. This view often causes extreme annoyance to other Christians, but I can only say that I have seen a number of cases where people's spiritual life was clouded until such things were renounced. In one case, a woman who had practised yoga before her conversion was unable to take communion, suffered from appalling shaking and other distressing symptoms until she was freed in the name of Christ.

But it is always important to remember that *many people think that they are demonized when they are not*. It is often seen as a way out for those suffering personality problems such as violence or sexual difficulties which are usually marks of the flesh. There are certain common marks of demonization – inability to pray even the Lord's Prayer, unwillingness to use the name of Jesus, violent reaction to Christian symbols such as the cross, or consecrated water or oil, sudden deafness when Scripture is read, tightly closed eyes or clenched hands when being prayed with, wild laughs and displays of physical strength. Nevertheless these are not 'litmus paper' tests, and such people may well be suffering from psychological disorders.

Contact with a church, or prayer group, may greatly accentuate the person's feeling of bondage. Just as the evil spirits shrieked at the sight of Jesus, so they may lie dormant for years, until a person has some religious contact.

This is emphatically not an area of ministry to get involved in lightly. No one should embark on prayer alone or without the covering of someone in spiritual authority. It is important, for instance, for Anglican clergy to submit to the authority of their bishops. Such ministry can be costly, and we need to pray for protection for everyone involved, and their families, from counter-attack. 'The angel of the Lord encamps around those who fear him' (Ps. 34.7) is a promise which has meant much to me.

It would be wrong to give the impression that deliverance ministry need be long or drawn out. Recently we have seen a number of cases which, though very real, were dealt with very quickly. Once, the sense of evil was so strong that one of the ministering team was knocked backwards. Even so, the total praying time was only about ten minutes, and the feeling of relief tremendous.

Finally, after such ministry, it is important to pray for the person to be filled with the Holy Spirit. In cases of deep occult involvement, there is a very strong, almost magnetic, pull back. In a few cases, I have known former 'friends' attempt to put curses upon people who have been delivered and to harm them (and us) in other ways.

The person who has been set free will need considerable support and love after experiencing such a deep spiritual battle within his or her personality. Nevertheless, after release, those ministered to are wonderfully grateful and will often want to join Charles Wesley in singing:

> I woke the dungeon flamed with light.
> My chains fell off, my heart was free,
> I rose, went forth, and followed Thee.

NOTES

1 See the discussion of Mark 1.24ff. in W. Lane, *The Gospel of Mark*, New London Commentaries (Marshall, Morgan & Scott), pp. 74ff.

2 Usually Jesus commanded the demons to be silent. We are most unwise to talk to the demons though occasionally they may name themselves.

3 This parable is a great warning. People with demonic problems have a tendency to return to darkness and if they do the last state is often worse than the first. This is sometimes caused by extreme pressure from former associates who will stop at nothing to get people back.

4 Jesus normally told demons to leave without specifying where. We have no warrant to do anything except send them to him.

5 In *Expository Thoughts on the Gospels* (J. Clarke).

6 See Acts 8.7; 16.16–18; 19.11–20; and Michael Green's *Evangelism in the Early Church* (Hodder & Stoughton), pp. 188ff.

7 See Michael Green, *I Believe in Satan's Downfall* (Hodder & Stoughton 1981) ch. 6. This book has a fuller discussion of the whole issue of demon possession.

7 Crisis

Paul, Silas and Timothy had just begun the second missionary journey. They had had two experiences of negative guidance (Acts 16.6ff), and then the great vision of a man of Macedonia beseeching them to come and preach there. Joined by Luke (note how the narrative suddenly changes to 'we'), they quickly arrived in Philippi. This was the capital of Macedonia, and the scene of a famous battle in 42 BC in which Anthony and Octavian (the future emperor Augustus) defeated Brutus and Cassius, the murderers of Julius Caesar.

Not long after they arrived, they were in trouble! For some days they had been pursued by a slave girl who cried out for money, 'These men are servants of the Most High!', until Paul could stand it no longer. He commanded the evil spirit to leave the girl and without further ado it did. (Having once experienced this sort of thing, Paul seems to me a model of patience. I only managed a few minutes before taking some sort of action.) Literally all hell was let loose. The slave girl's owners were furious. She brought them a fine profit with her utterances.

Then as now, messages from the spirit world were very much sought after and could be very accurate. Apart from anything else there is a deadly tendency towards self-fulfilment which partly explains the potency of such foretelling. I met a girl who had been told by a fortune teller that she would always be depressed, a prediction quite sufficient to keep her in bondage. On another celebrated occasion a witch arrived in our house apparently seeking help. She couldn't have known that Jane was due to go into labour that night (or indeed that she was pregnant – she had not yet seen her!). But in the midst of a mighty verbal conflict she declared, 'Your wife will go into labour tonight!' To which I replied, with uncharacteristic fervour, 'That is a lie – in the name of the Lord!' I've always believed that that is why Rachel, our oldest child, was born ten days later than expected.

People are always furious when Christianity brings financial loss. The makers of the silver images in Ephesus rioted (Acts 19) because their trade was disappearing. An anonymous writer in the *Gentleman's Magazine* attacked Wesley and Whitefield for preaching to the coal-miners in these lines:

The industry of the inferior people in a society is the great source of its prosperity. But if one man like Mr Whitefield should have by the power of his preaching to detain five or six thousands of the vulgar from their daily labour, what a loss in a little time may this bring to the public! For my part I shall expect to hear of a prodigious rise in the price of coals about the city of Bristol, if this gentleman proceeds as he has begun, with his charitable lectures to the colliers of Kingswood.

The parents of a boy whom I know, rounded on his public school headmaster. The trouble was that the lad had been converted and was considering ordination. They produced the immortal line, 'We haven't paid £2,000 a year for our son to become a clergyman!'

The slave girl's owners did more than complain. They dragged Paul and Silas before the magistrates. With commendable subtlety, they accused them not of exorcising their profitable slave girl, but of advocating customs which would be illegal for Romans to accept or to practise. They were perfectly correct in this – there were laws forbidding foreign religious propaganda amongst Roman citizens. Besides, anti-Jewish sentiment ran high in such places, and to any outsider Paul and Silas were merely propagating some rather extreme form of Judaism.

Summary justice was given. The magistrates used their right to inflict corporal punishment. Paul and Silas were severely beaten and flung into prison. The jailor interpreted his instructions to keep them safe in the strictest way possible – Paul and Silas, sore and bleeding, were secured in the stocks in the heart of the prison.

In this unpromising situation, they prayed and sang hymns! A number of rather facile comments are often made about this incident. Paul and Silas doubtless did count it a blessing that they had been considered worthy to suffer for Jesus, but one doubts if they gave praise for their unjust conviction and the apparent reduction of Christian missionary work. Jesus wept at injustice and forthcoming calamity, he did not give praise! We are called to 'rejoice in the Lord always' (Phil. 4.4) but not necessarily to rejoice at what we see and experience.

There must have been something deeply disturbing about the hymns and prayers from within the prison cell. Small wonder that the other prisoners listened. Geoffrey Bull, in his book *When Iron Gates Yield*, tells of his thrill when we heard a

Christian hymn being sung in another part of the prison. Richard Wurmbrand, in *In God's Underground*, tells of many wonderful experiences amidst the torture and treachery of the Rumanian prisons. His own survival, including recovering without drugs or proper vitamins from tuberculosis, is as remarkable as the events in Philippi.

Paul, a great man of prayer, was also a man of praise! And soon there was a cause for both terror and rejoicing!

An earthquake, a not uncommon phenomenon in those parts, shook the foundations of the prison, broke their fetters, and blasted open the prison doors. The jailor, probably a retired Roman soldier, awoke, and assumed that the prisoners had escaped. The crisis was unbearable and he prepared to take the honourable and expected course of action – suicide.

Paul, sensing what was happening, called out to him to desist. None of the prisoners had escaped, despite the doors being wide open. The startled jailor asked the classic question 'Men, what must I do to be saved?'

John Wesley records an incident with certain similarities which happened at Shepton Mallet.

Feb: 1748 – After preaching at Oakhill, about noon, I rode to Shepton Mallet, and found them under all manner of strange consternation. A mob, they said, was hired, prepared and made sufficiently drunk, in order to do all manner of mischief. I began preaching between 4 and 5, none hindered or interrupted at all, and the hearts of many were comforted. I wondered what was become of the mob, but we were quickly informed they mistook the place imagining that I should alight (as I used to do) at William Stone's house, and had summoned by drum all their forces to meet me at my coming. But Mr Swindells innocently carrying me into the other end of the town they did not discover their mistake till I had left off preaching. So the hindering of this, which was one of their designs was utterly disappointed.

However, they followed us from the preaching house to William Stone's, throwing dirt, stones and clods. But they could not hurt us, only Mr Swindells had a little dirt on his coat, and I had a few specks on my hat.

After we had gone into the house, they began throwing great stones, in order to break the door, but perceiving that this would require some time they dropped that design for the present. They first broke all the tiles on the penthouse over the door, and then poured a shower of stones at the windows. One of their leaders had followed us with great zeal, into the house and was now shut in with us. He did not like this, and would fain have got out, but this was not possible. So he kept as close to me as he could, thinking himself safe when he was near me; but staying a little behind when I went up two flights of stairs, a large stone stuck him on the forehead. He cried out 'Oh sir, are we to die tonight? What must I do? What must I do?' I said 'Pray to God. He is able to deliver you from all danger!' He took my advice and began praying in a manner such as he had scarce done ever since he was born.

We don't know what ultimately happened to the man. In Paul's case, the end was clear. The jailor may not have intended as much by his question, but he received a full gospel answer from Paul. 'Believe in the Lord Jesus, and you will be saved, and your household.' He took them home, got the family up and listened to his first sermon! Then he washed their wounds, they washed him and his family in baptism, and then they all had a meal together. The evening finished with much rejoicing – and doubtless more hymn singing!

The jailor is the archetypal example of a 'crisis' conversion. Christian history abounds with stories of those who were saved only because they endured some terrible physical or emotional crisis.

John Newton, famous preacher and hymn writer of the eighteenth century, was for many years a slave trader. Brought up to know the Bible, he had become an evil blaspheming man. Even hardened slave traders regarded him with some suspicion. In the midst of a terrible storm, he was nearly cast overboard as the ship's Jonah. Later he sought God and promised to live a new way if he survived. Amazingly the ship survived, they didn't die of starvation or thirst, and John Newton kept his promise! He knew what love meant when he wrote the hymn

> Amazing grace that saved a wretch like me
> I once was lost, but now am found . . .

A most moving modern example of crisis conversion was told in a sermon by George Hoffman, Director of TEAR fund. A missionary had to leave Vietnam because of the imminent defeat of the South Vietnamese by the communists. He still longed to be used to convert Vietnamese. As he settled in Hong

Kong he continued to pray . . . An army officer fell foul of the regime in Vietnam. He was imprisoned, escaped and longed to get out of the country. He began praying to an unknown God. Eventually he escaped on a crowded refugee boat. Then disaster struck. Lashed by a heavy storm, the overloaded craft drifted helplessly. Looking at the many women and young children, he prayed to the unknown God to protect them. Suddenly the boat seemed guided through the storm. They arrived in Hong Kong; he was met by the missionary and quickly was converted. And the missionary began to see many more Vietnamese conversions for his labours!

I met a man in Oxford, whose life had hit the rocks. His second marriage had ended in divorce (his first wife had died), he had left his teaching post, and was without a job, money or hope. He found counsel and friendship at St Aldate's. He became a believer, joined an early morning prayer group, and found a job – reading gas meters. Life trudged on. Though prospects in British Gas were not exactly thrilling, he was grateful to the Lord for work, but lonely and unfulfilled. Then quite suddenly, the idea of ordination gripped him. By a strange set of circumstances, he started to meet his ex-wife regularly. Soon they were remarried, and he was accepted for ordination training. About four years after the initial crisis, he was ordained and rejoicing in the wonderful new task that he had been given.

A young girl lay in an Oxford hospital. Some years earlier she had been almost killed in a motor cycle accident, which had led to a rather hasty marriage to the man who was driving it. She drifted into drugs and promiscuous sex, and many of her friends were deep into witchcraft. For a short time, she had lived in south Oxford, next door to a Christian family with a great gift for hospitality. Through them, she'd been to one or two Bible studies. Now in hospital; depressed and suffering from mild doses of heroin, she was visited by two Christians. They didn't know her, but her former neighbour had put them on to her. She hid under the bedclothes, and tried not to listen to them. But they persisted in visiting her. She was intrigued, and after she had left hospital, started to visit their church. On her first visit she was converted. Although there were many difficult years ahead, she became a faithful disciple, and particularly gifted in helping others in deep trouble.

In some situations, and for some people, it seems that only a crisis can enable God's voice to be heard. Charles Colson was one of the toughest men in President Nixon's government. A more unlikely convert – let alone evangelist – could scarcely be imagined. But, caught up in the Watergate scandal, he was sent to prison and his political career was ruined. In the midst of this disaster, Christ met him and he was brought to faith. Now he works for the welfare of prisoners and uses every opportunity to proclaim his new-found faith.

A different sort of crisis enabled Watchman Nee and a team of Chinese evangelists to get through to a group of off-shore islanders. At first, they were totally uninterested in the Christian message. They were quite happy worshipping their local god – Ta-Wang. They saw no need of Jesus. Besides, it was Ta-Wang's festival next week. It would be a fine day, as it always had been, and they would have a great celebration. One young Christian boldly announced that it would rain on the day of the god's festival. The rest of the team were somewhat alarmed. Had they been presumptuous? Would God honour their somewhat rash statement? The weather looked set fair. As they prayed, the word came 'Remember the God of Elijah'. Encouraged, they continued their evangelistic campaign. On the day of the festival, the Christians rose early and prayed to God. Very soon it started to rain and soon there was a spectacular downpour.

The diviners associated with Ta-Wang said that they had got the day wrong and announced a new date for the ceremonies. The Christians calmly said it would be fine until the day of the festival when it would rain again! When this happened, many of the islanders forsook Ta-Wang and turned to Christ.

Watchman Nee, in his book *Sit, Walk and Stand*, records how years later he met the young Christian who had first issued the challenge over the weather. He was now an airline pilot. 'Do you remember . . . ?' asked Watchman Nee.

'How could I forget?' replied the man.

Yet people are not always converted by signs. The psychologist's husband who was at dinner with us (see Chapter 6), when the table was overturned had just been talking about his need to see an act of God. He was impressed, remains friendly and sympathetic to our work, but as yet hasn't joined the Church.

Obviously crises do not always bring people to faith. Indeed some people turn away from God when faced with adversity or tragedy. Sadly, too, while there are many stories of conversions and Christian heroism in times of persecution, there are also

71

those who fall away. None of us knows how we will react in such circumstances. Jesus has warned all of us that we will face many difficulties. He didn't promise us immunity from disease or accident. We would be wise to remember this in the good times, so that our faith is not destroyed in time of trouble.

I am constantly impressed by the testimony of many believers as to how their faith has helped them in times of sudden tragedy, illness or bereavement.

Thus we have seen in this chapter, and elswhere, many examples of people finding faith during, or soon after, some dark moment in their lives. A crisis sharpens the mind, and pierces the soul – for some the response will be anger, despair, and an apparently final rejection of God; for others it is the great turning-point when darkness and despair turns to light and joy.

So much depends upon the help they receive. For those of us in more normal circumstances, our task is to pray, keep our eyes open so that we are available to help, and if called upon to do so 'to account for the hope that is within us' (1 Pet. 3.15).

One final word. We must remember the parable of the sower. 'Some seed fell on rocky ground, where it had not much soil . . . and since it had no root it withered away' (Mark 4.5,6).

People who have come to faith through great crisis have very wonderful testimonies. They are often eager 'to declare the wonderful deeds of him who called you out of darkness into his marvellous light' (1 Peter 2.9). That is good, but it can be overdone. Too much publicity, too much testimony, can weaken the roots. Problems like alcoholism, drug addiction, occult involvement, do not go away easily. People with such experiences will need a great deal of sensitive care. The Church should avoid the temptation to parade them around as 'God's latest miracle'.

8 *At Home*

'Come to my house and stay' (Acts 16.15).

I well remember, in my unmarried days, preaching one Sunday in a large church in a neighbouring city. I hadn't organized myself any lunch and was hoping that something would turn up! After preaching enthusiastically and talking to a number of people, it was time to leave. The vicar came up to say goodbye. 'My wife says that I should have asked you to lunch.' I smiled encouragingly. He continued, 'Do drop in the next time you're in our city'. I wonder what his reaction would have been if I'd called for a seven o'clock breakfast with my wife after getting off the local car ferry!

By way of contrast, most Christians are very generous and open-hearted about the use of their homes. Hospitality is one of the great New Testament marks of grace. The pages of Scripture are full of examples of hospitality and exhortations to practise it.

When Paul and his companions first arrived in Philippi (see the previous chapter), they looked for someone with whom they could have fellowship in worship. Eventually, on the Jewish Sabbath, they found a place of prayer. Some women gathered together, amongst them Lydia who was involved in the important trade of selling purple-coloured cloth. Purple, the imperial colour, was mainly acquired from the murex sea snail. Lydia seems to have been a person of some means, personally acquired from this profitable commercial enterprise. She is also described as a worshipper of God. Like Cornelius (Acts 10) she was seeking for clearer revelation, and was only too glad to be directed towards Jesus. (Such an attitude is in sharp contrast to those who today claim to believe in God, usually as a defence against real commitment to Christ. C.S. Lewis is one of the relatively few well-known converts who first became a God fearer, and then quickly saw that this must lead to Jesus.) Anyway, the Lord 'opened Lydia's heart' – the normal New Testament emphasis on the saving work beginning with God and not man – and she listened attentively to Paul. Soon afterwards, she and all her household were baptized. Then she urged the four travellers to come and stay at her home.

This practical action gave Paul and his companions a sound base from which to build up their evangelistic work in Philippi. Lydia, and her household, must have benefited spiritually, and grown in faith, as a result of seeing how the missionaries lived and prayed.

Later, after their unfortunate arrest and subsequent deliverance through the earthquake, Paul and Silas experienced more hospitality, this time in the prison jailor's home. The jailor's action brought blessing to himself and his whole household. 'They spoke the word of the Lord to him and to all that were in his house . . . he was baptized at once, with all his family' (Acts 16.32–3).

It speaks much for Paul's sense of priority that, despite the pain of their wounds and inevitable hunger, they first preached the gospel, then had their backs washed and ate a meal.

The jailor took a risk in entertaining Paul, as events showed the next day, when the magistrates tried to get Paul out of the city. But it cannot be a coincidence that Philippi, where homes were opened so readily, seems also to have been the happiest of the New Testament churches to which Paul wrote.

I have often noticed how generous many Christians become in the use of their homes. Becoming a Christian household affects many things – the state of the house, the attitude to neighbours and strangers, and the children.

I remember one household which when I first visited was an absolute 'tip'. Nobody cared for house or garden, and meals were also casual and irregular. The children looked sad and frightened. Then very gradually, as the whole family started 'growing up to salvation' the home changed. The house became tidy, flowers appeared in the garden and indoors, neighbours started to drop in, and the gospel was shared over cups of tea and coffee.

Another household stands out in my memory. The wife was not a strong person, quite often ill and with a difficult baby, yet her house was often full. People would park their kids there, other would come for coffee, more for advice and prayer. In addition, they led a Christian group which met in their home, and took a full part in the political and social life around. Her husband, apart from having a very demanding job, was one of the local church leaders. At first, he and I often clashed at meetings. I was somewhat afraid of him, and I suppose annoyed that anyone questioned my thinking! Gradually I recognized that frequently he spoke with God-given wisdom, and as his voice became heard, so it seemed to become softer! A number of families and individuals have grown spiritually and emotionally as a result of the friendship and open doors of this household.

Similarly other households, often with very little space, opened their doors and took in people to stay who were either in temporary or long-term difficulties. Sometimes these arrangements didn't work, and brought a lot of heartache, but the intention was good.

The idea of 'extended' households has become very fashionable in some Christian circles. In a typical household, a Christian couple and their children form the basic unit and take in one or two additional single people. This helps the economics of the family, provides a home base for some single people, and forms a praying unit for the local church.

This sounds marvellous in theory and has worked well in some churches both at home and abroad. But one shouldn't underestimate the tensions that can arise. Single people don't always appreciate dirty nappies and crying children, families don't find it easy to adjust to lack of space and much less privacy.

One thing I have learnt, through seeing such households in turmoil, is that any extended family needs a small group of outside praying partners. These can advise about membership of the household and help with any other problems which arise. It is very hard for the head of a household to be objective about someone else coming to stay – an outside group can be far wiser and thus help to prevent future disasters . . .

Ideally such households could become places of . . . refuge for the weak, underprivileged members of a church family. In practice, many extended families are completely wrecked by starry-eyed idealism about the sort of people who can be helped. Recent converts, especially, would be wiser to follow the examples of Lydia and the jailor and use any extra rooms to support mature Christian workers. Later on, as their faith and experience grows, they can step out into the much more difficult field of supporting those with deeper needs.

On a more ordinary level, Christians can use their homes in a wide variety of ways. One couple that I know entertained a large number of their friends to tell them about a mission which was happening in their church. Then, at the actual time of the mission, they invited them all a second time. Most of them came back, and eventually some time subsequent to the actual mission, one couple was converted.

Obviously hospitality is not a specifically Christian virtue, but it is an area of great pastoral opportunity. New Christians benefit immensely from evenings out with more established church members, and they can also very quickly learn to use their own houses in the Lord's service.

One church encouraged its members to set aside a weekday evening to entertain fellow members and neighbours. Obviously such a policy is costly both in time and money, but a meal together establishes a quality of relationship which is not easily obtainable in any other way.

The other great effect on Lydia and the jailor was on their households. We are not told what family they had, but in each case their households were baptized (and presumably believed!). Indeed, Paul specifically promised the jailor that he and his household would be saved. Similarly, in the gospel story (Luke 19.1–10), after Zaccheus' dramatic act of repentance, Jesus said to him, 'Today salvation has come to this house.' What did Jesus mean? How could Zaccheus' repentance affect his household?

Of course, he would set a better example, he would live a better life. But Jesus meant far more than that. So did Paul when he said to the jailor, 'Believe . . . and you will be saved, you and your household.' So did Peter when he preached at the first Pentecost (Acts 2.39): 'The promise is to you and to your children and to all that are far off, every one whom the Lord calls to him.'

Their expectation was combined in the familiar Old Testament belief in family solidarity. This is clearly expressed in Psalm 103.17: 'But the steadfast love of the Lord is from everlasting to everlasting, upon those who fear him, and his righteousness to children's children.' This verse (a great promise particularly appropriate at the funeral service of an aged believer), acts as a commentary upon the third commandment (Exod. 20.6). God's love extends down the generations of the righteous.

This has important implications for the upbringing of the children of Christian parents. One Christian leader, himself an effective evangelist, told me that his prayer for his children had been that they would never need to see the day of conversion.

His hope was that they would gradually grow into faith without a wilderness period of rebellion and unbelief. His prayer seems to have been fully answered as all his children are committed Christians, several in full-time Christian service. It was a delight to visit his family, and sense the unity and love of the whole household.

I can think of a number of other Christian families with a similar testimony. Of course in each case the appropriation of faith is unique. Some children do experience a decisive moment of repentance and receiving Jesus; others just become gradually aware that he is their Lord and the director of their young lives. Thus, our hope and prayer should be that our children will grow up as faithful disciples. Equally, we understand that in the mystery of God's sovereignty and their free will, this is no certainty. But a firm belief that they are within God's Kingdom until they opt out, will protect us from pressurizing them to take 'decisions'. It makes us as parents less anxious about their future and more relaxed in facing up to their questions and doubts.

I well remember Rachel at four and a half, saying at Easter time, 'Is it really really *really* true that Jesus rose from the dead?' Another little girl, aged about four, told me that she didn't say prayers because she didn't know Jesus yet. What sort of parental theology gives children that impression? An old man died, apparently full of atheism and hostility to Christ, largely because he had been terrified of God through having hell preached to him at the age of five. I knew him well, he was wonderfully educated, a delightful man, an expert on the religious paintings in Venice, and yet perhaps the most convinced atheist whom I have ever met.

All of this may well have implications for our baptismal policy. If we believe that our children are holy (that is 'set apart' by God, not necessarily little angels!) (1 Cor. 7.14), we shall want them to be baptized. We shall act in faith, believing that God's grace is at work unseen. If we believe that our children are dead in their trespasses (Eph. 2.1), we shall certainly not want them baptized until they are old enough to profess conversion. On no account shall we encourage the routine baptism of unbelievers' children. This, however, is easier said than done! In the last resort, we are not called to judge. The duty of the Church, and church members must help and support their clergy in this, is to proclaim the faith, warn parents of the futility of purely formal baptisms, and to see interviews with parents bringing children for baptism as one of the primary opportunities for preaching the gospel.

Any church which fails to provide reasonable teaching for children, and crèche facilities for the very young, has only itself to blame that few young families are seen amongst its worshippers.

In the three biblical narratives we have considered, we are reminded of the importance that God places upon the head of the household. An elderly Chilean lady became a Christian at the age of eighty. She said to the man who helped her to faith, 'I've wasted so much of my life – what can I do with the rest of it?' He replied, 'Pray, especially for those members of your family whom God particularly lays upon your heart'. She prayed for two of her grandchildren. One quickly became a Christian and is now a clergyman's wife. The other was a student drop-out. He was challenged, but outwardly unmoved, by his cousin's lifestyle. In Spain for a holiday, he was walking one afternoon towards Avila. Suddenly God spoke to him clearly and directly. He became a disciple. The last thing his grandmother was able to do before she died, at the age of about ninety, was to attend his ordination. He now has a tremendous ministry in Chile, not least amongst the rest of her extensive family.

The importance of the Christian family cannot be over exaggerated. It stands as an important beacon of light, amidst the shaking society around us. As the foundations of the family are shaken by secular attacks on marriage, faithfulness, and the like, so God's blessing on families seems more evident. I am convinced that we should expect to see whole families converted and unitedly learning to serve the Lord. I have seen marriages rescued when both partners have experienced conversion.

Woe betide those who minister, or exercise positions of church leadership, and ignore their wives and families. Paul recognized the wisdom of the Apostles being accompanied by their wives (1 Cor. 9.5); he also stressed on several occasions the importance of Christian leaders' families (e.g. Titus 1.6), something which the current jet set of Christian leaders might do well to copy. Every Christian's first field of ministry is in his home. If we are too busy to teach our children to pray, to read them Bible stories, and to enjoy their company in other ways,

78

then we are too busy.

We need too to guard our homes. Constant open doors are unsettling for the children. Occasionally, we must draw back and unashamedly spend time together as a family. Children too should be consulted, especially if we are considering forming extended households or have lengthy visitations. Their friends need to be invited, and their needs watched.

A happy home is a wonderful base from which to work. The minister, or Christian leader, whose home expresses the peace and joy of God, is truly fortunate. It is the greatest encouragement to labour long and hard, if we know that what we are doing is appreciated and understood. Within limits, work experiences should be shared with all the family. Even the youngest can have a keen sense of good and evil, and a keen sense of God's power.

Paul had received three sorts of hospitality in Philippi. Gracious living with the prosperous Lydia, the penitential stocks of the Imperial prison, and emergency treatment at the jailor's household. What next? The rest is something of an anticlimax. The magistrates, considerably alarmed, gave instructions for the release of Paul and Silas. Paul retorted that he was a Roman citizen, who had been grossly mistreated. He demanded a personal meeting. The magistrates, suitably deflated, came and made personal apology. Then they asked Paul to leave. He probably insisted on protection for the church, then said farewell to Lydia and the rest of the church, and went on towards Thessalonica.

Apparently they left Luke behind (see Acts 16.40 and cf. Acts 20.5), and the church flourished. Certainly Paul's letter to the Philippians, and his other references to the generous Macedonians (2 Cor. 8.1, 2 Cor. 9.2, Rom. 15.26), make it clear that this was one of the happiest churches which he founded. He made a brief visit on his way back to Jerusalem (Acts 20.1–6) and clearly found much to encourage him. Luke rejoined him there and accompanied him all the way to prison in Rome.

And the memory of the Philippian church remained a constant source of joy and encouragement to Paul (Phil. 1.3ff). They continued to send gifts to him – a fragrant offering, a sacrifice acceptable and pleasing to God (Phil. 4.18). Generosity and hospitality were hallmarks of this joyful congregation. Some of the life of this little church must have revolved around

Lydia whose gentle crisis had led to the opening of a home base for Paul, and around the jailor who had so dramatically started growing up to salvation. Their two households must have provided a marvellous base from which the new church could expand.

9 *Guidance*

'An angel of the Lord said to Philip . . .' (Acts 8.26).

Philip was chosen as one of seven deacons, to serve the church by helping in the distribution of food and money to the poor. The Greek widows had felt aggrieved; they were convinced that their Jewish counterparts were getting a better deal, and so they complained. Wisely, the Apostles acted quickly to snuff out this grumbling. They instructed the church to choose seven men, 'full of the Spirit and of wisdom, of good repute' to do the practical work while the Apostles concentrated on their primary calling to prayer and preaching (Acts 6.1–6). Philip was one of those selected.

What did it mean to be 'full of the Spirit'? It was invariably true that new disciples received the Spirit upon conversion (the only real recounted exception to this is in the Samaritan city in which Philip preached, see Acts 8.4–17); nevertheless the fullness of the Spirit was something that it was possible to lose, or never to attain.

The Galatian Christians, converts of Paul and Barnabas's first missionary journey, were rebuked by Paul for beginning with the Spirit, and ending with the flesh (Gal. 3). They had set out on a path guided and led by the Spirit (Gal. 5.16–26), but had slipped back into a formal legalistic discipleship. They had effectively quenched the power of the Spirit within themselves and their church (1 Thess. 5.19).

The Ephesian churches were instructed by Paul to be continuously filled with the Spirit (Eph. 5.18). This wasn't some distant empowering experience of long ago (which they may well have had), but a continuous ongoing experience of the Spirit's leading.

One mark of the fullness of the Spirit is a tremendous sense of the love of God. To return for a moment to the metaphor of the L-shaped field, it is a time when we move out of the shadows of the trees into the blazing light of the sun. There is a definite sense of purpose, an awareness of warmth, and an appreciation of the vastness of the field and the greatness of God's purposes.

I heard an archbishop speaking in St Aldate's of his own initial experience. He was reading a Sunday newspaper when he felt a compelling urge to put it down and go and enter his private chapel. There he just knelt prostrate under a sense of the Spirit's power and warmth. God's love, so broad and wide, so high and deep, poured over him, transforming his faith and expectation.

Some of my teaching colleagues laughed when the headmaster put up a notice saying: 'John Woolmer is appointed chaplain with immediate effect.' Most of them didn't know that a small mission was beginning that day, which paved the way for more effective evangelism subsequently.

Philip was a man with immediate effect! Doubtless he and the others dealt with the widows graciously and properly. Then Stephen, another of the seven, got down to the business of preaching with such explosive results, that he was run in by the Sanhedrin. Very quickly, he was given a short trial, and stoned to death. Saul of Tarsus, who watched approvingly, launched a vicious attack upon the church. He broke into homes, zealously carrying both men and women into prison. Most of the Christians were scattered and fled.

Philip and others, however, turned this catastrophe to good advantage. They went and preached in a much wider area, thereby fulfilling the next stage of the Ascension Day charge: 'You shall be my witnesses in Jerusalem and in all Judea and Samaria and to the end of the earth' (Acts 1.8).

A sense of the Spirit's guidance is another frequent mark amongst those who are filled with the Spirit. Sometimes this guidance is spectacular, and Philip's later ministry will illustrate this; at other times it is a matter of using circumstances intelligently.

Philip began preaching in a Samaritan city – with dramatic effect! Crowds listened to him, and saw his preaching authenticated by the normal Kingdom signs of healing and exorcism. The people received his teaching gladly, and there was much joy in the city. Very soon there were queues for baptism. This dramatic, and successful, ministry came to a sudden end when an angel of the Lord summoned Philip to go some miles south and wait on the Jerusalem–Gaza road.

It is easy to mock such tales of guidance. We enjoy stories like the one of the clergyman who, bored with a diocesan conference, left after lunch. On the way out, he met the Bishop. 'The Holy Spirit has told me to do a little shopping', said the man blandly. 'And did the Holy Spirit tell you it was early closing day?' retorted the Bishop.

I remember, too, after I had attended a public healing meeting to receive prayer on behalf of someone else, an earnest lady assuring me that the Lord had told her that I'd been healed!

But for all the problems, there are many wonderful direct testimonies of clear guidance. One thing is certain, if the guidance comes by revelation from God it will be crystal clear and the end result will be important. The angel would not have guided Philip on to an empty desert road.

Once I spent about six months looking for the right job. I was sure that it was right to leave my current one, and I began to look for the appropriate situation. Various openings came, but none of them felt right. Guidance in this case was indirect and intuitive. Then suddenly I had to come to a decision. Three possible churches were interested in me; two had offered me the job, a third was considering doing so. I had kept one waiting a long time, and now I had to decide.

God spoke in three ways. First, when we applied for one of the posts, we received a polite but firm refusal from the patron – they had plenty of good candidates. A little while later we spent an evening with a couple whom we had asked especially to pray about our future. After much talk, and some prayer, James said: 'Father is saying that you will find something significant in the next week.' The next day, Jane received a phone call from the churchwardens of the church that had plenty of candidates asking me to go for an interview! We were offered that job.

Then God spoke again. We had gathered together a group of our friends and leaders in the church which we were leaving. There was a general, but not complete, consensus as to which job was right, then our parish worker saw a picture in her mind of a long, low, grey stone house. It didn't mean much to me, but Jane said, 'It's the rectory at . . .' The next morning James rang up with a long word of prophecy. The words which stood out were that we were to 'choose this day the church which was right for us as a family, and the church where we could serve the whole community as well as the church'. The church with the grey stone rectory was far more suited to the family in terms of potential friends and situation, and it was a town parish church, whereas the other possibilities had congregations gathered from afar. There was far more opportunity to serve in the community from the centre of a town parish. For final confirmation, I rang up a bishop involved in the appointment of one of the other potential jobs. He listened, then said quietly, 'I also know the parish with the grey stone rectory. That's where you should go!' In some ways it wasn't the natural choice, the churchmanship being rather different from what we were used to, but the prophetic words also mentioned that 'We would be changed', which seemed to cover that point as well. We felt at peace; six months of waiting were over! When on the night of our induction our former parish worker actually saw the house, she gasped. It was exactly the house she had seen in her mind!

Philip's guidance was somewhat less involved. A quick command from an angel to be in a certain place at a certain time. An angel? Do they really exist?

Kenneth McAll (see chapter 5), in his pre-war days as a missionary in China, was walking towards a desert village. He had already had one narrow escape when arrested and tried by the invading Japanese. As he walked, a man joined him and asked him to change direction and go to a different village. He turned and accompanied the man to their destination. When they arrived, the villagers were delighted and said they needed plenty of help. 'But why did you change direction?' they asked. 'You were walking towards a village which we think is occupied by the Japanese.' They said they had watched him walking in the desert, but had seen no man stop and talk to him. When Kenneth looked around there was no trace of the man. It was then that he realized that his guide had spoken to him in English!

For Philip, confirmation of the angel's guidance came when an Ethiopian, a senior court official, came down the road in his chariot. He was even reading, aloud, from the scriptures! The significance of that meeting is the subject of the next chapter. For the moment suffice to say that it led to the conversion of the Ethiopian. After that encounter, Philip was whisked away and found himself some twenty miles to the north, in Azotus.

Philip made his way up the coast and settled at Caesarea. There he, and his daughters who prophesied, entertained Paul on his way to Jerusalem (Acts 21.8). It was quite a prophetic household; before Paul had been there long Agabus turned up from Judea. He had once before foretold a severe famine (Acts 11.28) and caused the Antioch church to take action to relieve the Judean Christians. Now, with fine Old Testament symbolism, he removed Paul's girdle, binding his feet and hands, prophesying that Paul would be bound and delivered into the hands of the Gentiles. The company were much dismayed, but Paul told them to have heart. He had already told the Ephesian elders (Acts 20.23) that he was going to face considerable perils in Jerusalem, and he certainly wasn't going to shrink back.

This foretelling type of prophecy is rare in the Bible. The prophetic word usually foretold the general will for a situation, as for example when the church at Antioch some years earlier was guided to send Paul and Barnabas on their missionary journey (Acts 13. 1–3; see also Chapter 9).

Prophecy has been used to warn Christians of impending persecution. Christian tradition tells us that, around AD 67, a prophecy warned the Christian church in Jerusalem of the forthcoming siege by the Romans. The Christian community fled, thereby confirming the break with the Jewish leaders.

In more recent times, as recounted by Demos Shokarian in *The Happiest People on Earth*, a prophecy to the Armenian Christians some 120 years ago warned them of a fierce persecution by the Turks. The original prophecy was given by an illiterate boy of eleven in about 1850. About fifty years later, the prophet announced that the time of fulfilment was near. 'We must flee to America, all who remain here will perish.' The instructions proved correct. In 1914 a period of unimaginable horror arrived in Armenia. With ruthless efficiency, the Turks exterminated the Armenians. Their pogrom even inspired Hitler. 'The world did not intervene when Turkey wiped out the Armenians,' he reminded his followers, 'it will not intervene now.' Those who heeded the prophecy emigrated to America, those who stayed were almost all killed.

Of course, prophecy can get out of hand. Like any spiritual gift it can be perverted, and the scriptures are full of warning against, and examples of, false prophecy. The *Didache*, an early Christian handbook, has some trenchant advice: 'If a prophet claiming to be in a trance says give me money, he is not a true prophet of God!'

In my own experience, in church affairs we have been helped once or twice by prophecy. In 1980, as St Aldate's faced great uncertainties about reordering the interior of the church, as well as massive repair bills, a word of prophecy from an ex-member of the Parochial Church Council who had just moved away was a great help. It spoke specifically of the necessary money being provided, and of the need to reorder the church.

Once during a mission in a school, I felt that I should prophesy (something that has hardly ever happened to me). The only trouble was that we were saying Anglican Matins at 7.30 a.m.! The word seemed to be about arrows, and I asked the Lord for confirmation. I was directed to a page in the Psalter, and the first verse on the page was about arrows. The word was very simply about God's word being like an arrow, which must not be deflected, and which would accomplish its purpose. Anyway the evangelist was grateful and it gave him encouragement for his final address.

At the beginning of this chapter, we noticed that Philip's first move was guided largely by circumstances. We ought to consider what one might call the more normal and less exotic means of guidance.

Frequently, one just has a sense of peace that a particular pathway is right. Once, when a number of us were unhappy about the way our church fellowship groups were developing, we met to talk and to pray, and quite suddenly a new plan emerged. It seemed clearly right to all of us, and a deep, peaceful sense of unity surrounded us.

In church councils, we practically never vote – except occasionally to establish a preference on some unimportant matter. Major decisions require virtual unanimity. I remember once wanting to introduce a parish lunch. This I felt could be a key to improving our fellowship. Most of the people present were in favour, but a minority of about a quarter of those present were unhappy. We didn't go forward, and subsequent events suggested that the minority had probably been right.

Recently St Matthew's faced a major question of repairing the whole floor of the church. A massive sum for a small church, £16,000, would be needed. Despite generous help from St Aldate's, there was still a lot of money to be found. The architect advised quick action as he feared that prices would escalate soon. We called a parish meeting. To the astonishment of the architect, we received promises that night of loans and gifts which would cover the immediate cost. The decision to go ahead was not unanimous, one or two people expressing concern at such expenditure on our own needs, but on this occasion we had to take a decision. To do nothing would have been as decisive an action as to rebuild. The rebuilding went amazingly well, actually costing less than the minimum estimates, and the church is now used by another congregation in the evening in addition to the normal services.

Sometimes God seems to allow us to make apparent mistakes in order to teach us important lessons. The first theological college that I went to was a mistake (for me). One of my closest spiritual advisors had told me that it would be, and he was proved right!

One important experience, while I was there, was used to destroy my self-pity! One Sunday morning, I felt peculiarly miserable. My family life had disintegrated; my mother had just died and my father was far from well. I had been assigned by the college to do some visiting in the main hospital. As it happened, my lot was the cancer ward. I didn't know what to say to people. I was feeling utterly depressed and stupid . . .

The first person I talked to was very cheerful. She pointed out a young woman in the opposite corner – 'You must visit her'. Everyone said the same; eventually I reached the young woman. She was radiant! Very ill, yet utterly composed, and full of interest and encouragement. My own depression seemed so ridiculous, and insignificant. Her joy dispersed my self-pity and remains a memory to this day.

A friend of ours changed jobs and moved away from Oxford. Never exactly a convinced Anglican, he felt led to join a very different sort of church. The next six months were very difficult for him and his family. The church was far from ideal and eventually he moved back to the local Anglican church. But he had learnt to appreciate a lot of things that he'd taken for granted before. His discipleship, and usefulness, will have been deepened by the wilderness months.

Sometimes guidance from the Holy Spirit can change the direction of a meeting. I attended one of our house groups; they were planning to go away for a weekend, but everyone was in a scratchy and difficult mood. The weekend didn't look like being a success. I had a strong sense that God wanted the group to repent of their rebellious attitudes. A biblical reference came to mind; I opened the Bible – it was all about repentance! As I waited for an opportunity to speak, the girl next to me pointed to another biblical verse to which she had been led, also calling for repentance. The effect of sharing this with the meeting was devastating. Everyone, including some normally very silent group members, prayed prayers of repentance. The weekend was a great success.

Claiming special inspiration when preaching can be unwise! I've heard as many bad sermons claiming the direct inspiration of the Spirit as produced in any other ways. However my judgement isn't infallible! I heard one preacher tell how God had woken him up at two o'clock and given him this completely new sermon. I thought it was pretty awful! But when a very influential visitor was converted, I rather had to eat my words.

Guidance through mental pictures needs especial care. Someone at a prayer meeting saw a picture of a rose with two black spots. One person promptly interpreted this as saying that our policy on infant baptism was wrong! Knowing that this was one of his hobby horses, this interpretation was rejected. Nothing else was forthcoming, so the picture was put on one side, and the meeting continued. This is important, as otherwise such pictures can be a terrible distraction. At the end of the meeting a young girl came up and said it applied to her. Apparently a radiant Christian, she had deep troubles from the past which needed ministry. A Christian Science upbringing, some exposure to occult things abroad, lesbianism, and suicide attempts had left her very vulnerable to depressions and migraines.

Rather to our surprise, she manifested all the signs of demonization when we challenged anything evil in her to show itself. A long, and very difficult deliverance followed. At one moment a spirit started to speak through her and to name itself (this should, I think, be discouraged. Jesus usually commanded silence). We couldn't identify the name. An inner voice directed me to Zechariah 2.7. Feeling somewhat foolish I read out, 'Ho! Escape to Zion, you who dwell with the daughter of Babylon'. Michael Green, who was sharing the ministry with me, leapt to his feet. 'Of course! The Spirit's name is that of a Babylonic mystery religion.' Armed with this knowledge, the deliverance continued. This revelation, which needed both spiritual and scholastic insight, was key.

The story has a very happy ending. A while ago, not many years after the ministry, I conducted for this girl one of the happiest wedding services I've ever taken. The Lord is good!

Once, I was involved with others, in some difficult marital counselling. Some of us were getting depressed, as it seemed to absorb more and more time, and get more and more complicated. Then I received a picture. It was of two steep hillsides with a deep ravine between them. A stream ran through the ravine. At first the way was dark, but then the ravine opened out into a sunlit plain beyond. Two people were climbing the hills, one on each side.

The interpretation was simple! The couple were struggling forward, going towards the plain, in separate directions over steep and rough cliffs. What was required was a climbing down (mutual repentance) and a going through the ravine together. To begin with it would be dark, but soon it would broaden out in the fertile plain.

This helped me to believe that God would sort out the situation. It was a direction to minister to both people equally (which was necessary). We obeyed, and it is wonderful now to look back and see the outworking of the picture!

Sometimes the Spirit comes upon us, and leads us to pray with unusual faith. A woman who finds it quite hard to believe in answers to prayers, shared a difficulty she and her husband were having over a house purchase. This would bring them into the life of the parish, which was important for all of us as they did a lot of good work for the church. The problem was that the people selling the house to them had run into problems and the whole chain of buying and selling looked like snapping.

Another woman shared how her son was in lodgings with a Christian family who had a much smaller problem. Their children were being baptized the next day but both hated water and screamed when their hair was wetted!

We felt it right to pray about both matters. Within a few days the house purchase went through, and the children were baptized without a whimper. In fact, they even had a bath on the morning of the baptism and had their hair washed without a murmur!

One controversial situation is when X feels led by the Lord to tell Y what to do – usually unasked! I make it a rule to look for clear confirmation before embarking on such risky meddling in other people's lives. One of our leaders had a very sick baby. Although past the absolutely critical period, the baby was still doing badly and failing to put on weight. At one of our meetings, I felt convinced that the baby should be baptized. The only problem was that the family, for well-thought-out reasons, didn't believe in infant baptism! Then to my astonishment the mother suddenly said, 'I think the Lord is saying that James should be baptized!' I shared my thoughts. Her husband readily agreed. The baby seemed to get better from the moment that the decision was taken, and we had a memorable baptism. During the service another mother had a sort of visionary experience of an arc of light which lit up the faces of various members of the congregation; this was a help on her own Christian pilgrimage.

Sometimes I've had to take really big decisions without any clear leading. When the possibility of taking on the ministry at St Matthew's came up, it seemed the right thing to do. But no clear guidance came, one could only step out and hope! Often that is what God expects. In a way, we exercise more faith following flickering intuition into the unknown, than when we are zooming down a spiritual motorway lit by angelic lights. As in all else, the Spirit is sovereign. Sometimes he speaks very clearly, and at other times leaves us to search for the way.

There is a children's chorus[1] which expresses this sort of guiding experience. It, too, is an expression of great faith.

> I'm not alone for my Father is with me,
> With me wherever I go.
> Speaking words of faith, of courage, and of love,
> He's with me, he loves me, wherever I go.

This is so true. He's with me as I prepare for services (and sometimes one does feel that marvellous sense of inspiration and uplift), he's with me as I pray for others – often I've had to pray in faith with no particular sense of guidance and yet have discovered afterwards that the Father had been directing my words. He's with me when I visit, even on the black days when people are out, busy, or just uninterested. Occasionally they're downright insulting, and then I remember that Jesus, too, experienced that sort of rejection. He's with me as I go into sad situations – to the sick, the dying, the bereaved. And often his presence shines through other people's tears. He's with me as I enjoy the countryside or the family. And as I look back twelve years to the beginning of my second time at theological college, I can sense his amazing graciousness in all that he has given me. How well Plumptre puts it:

Thy hand, O God, has guided
Thy flock, from age to age.

NOTE

1 From *Fresh Sounds* by Betty Pulkingham (Hodder & Stoughton 1976).

10 *Scripture*

'The word of God is living and active, sharper than any two-edged sword' (Heb. 4.12).

As I was beginning to write this chapter, I asked a small group of Christians for their own testimony to the power of Scripture. I started a conversation which continued long after I had begun to write!

One, who had been a missionary in Nepal, recalled many examples of conversions in that country just through reading the Scriptures. In particular, there was a young man who was given a Bible, which he stuffed away in his trunk and ignored for two years. Then one day, feeling depressed, he settled down to read it and was immediately converted. Although it is no easy thing to become a Christian in Nepal, he became a faithful worshipper in the Church.

Two others spoke of friends converted in borstal or prison. In each case it was Bibles left in their cells that led the men to want to know more. One of them could scarcely read but was given the ability to read and understand a whole page of the Bible. This amazed him when he realized what had happened and underlined the power of what he was reading.

A fourth told me how she and her husband received very sudden news that they could have a baby for adoption in two days' time. This was distinctly awkward as they were due to go on holiday. One of their readings from *Daily Light*[1] was, 'Take this child away, and nurse him for me . . .' (Exod. 2.9). They adopted the baby, and forgot about their holiday!

A fifth mentioned seeking guidance as to whether it was right for him and his wife to leave Hong Kong and to join a Christian community in England. At the end of a meeting they were prayed for by someone who didn't know them. He read Isaiah 33.19–20. 'You will see no more . . . the people of an obscure speech. Your eyes will see Jerusalem, a quiet habitation, an immovable tent . . .' They had never mastered Chinese, it had always been 'obscure speech' to them. The great house, to which they were going if they joined the community, already had the vision of being a place of quiet for Christians to retreat to for prayer and peace.

Philip the evangelist, if he didn't know it already, discovered the direct power of Scripture, after the angel had directed him on to the Jerusalem–Gaza road (Acts 8; see Chapter 8 of this book). A chariot was coming down the road and its chief occupant was reading aloud from a scroll. And the words were very familiar! 'As a sheep led to the slaughter or a lamb before its shearers is dumb, so he opens not his mouth. In his humiliation justice was denied him. Who can describe his generation? For his life is taken up from the earth' (Isa. 53.7,8). The Ethiopian was reading a key passage of Scripture. He then asked a vital question. 'About whom, pray, does the prophet say this, about himself or about someone else?'

It is one of the signs that the Holy Spirit is preparing someone for conversion, or some other spiritual blessing, when they start to ask the vital questions. Philip doubtless continued reading from Isaiah the passage about the Suffering Servant that Christians have always seen as a prophecy of the Messiah. 'Surely he has borne our griefs and carried our sorrows; yet we esteemed him stricken, smitten by God, and afflicted. But he was wounded for our transgressions, he was bruised for our iniquities; upon him was the chastisement that made us whole, and with his stripes we are healed. All we like sheep have gone astray; we have turned every one to his own way; and the Lord has laid on him the iniquity of us all.'

Then, according to Acts, Philip told the Ethiopian the good news of Jesus. Presumably he told him first of the cross, and then of the resurrection; of the Church, and the signs and wonders which were confirming its work. He obviously also told him about baptism.

The eunuch was convinced and, like many men in positions of authority, once convinced he acted. Seeing some water, he stopped the chariot, and asked Philip to baptize him. Philip was only too happy to oblige. The waters poured over the Ethiopian symbolizing the death of the old life, and the beginning of the new.

Then, as suddenly as he had come, Philip was gone. The Ethiopian, the first individual recorded as being converted primarily through the witness of Scripture, went on his way rejoicing.

There are many known examples, throughout Christian history and in the present day, of the power of Scripture to open people's eyes. One modern instance is the story of Bilquis

Sheikh. She was a high-born Muslim, whose life collapsed when her husband, a high-ranking government official in Pakistan, left her. She retreated to the countryside looking for peace. But it eluded her. In her book, *I Dared to Call Him Father*, she records how, as she read the Koran, she found many references to the prophet Jesus. Out of curiosity she obtained a Bible and began to read: 'I will call them my people, which were not my people; and her beloved, which was not beloved. And it shall come to pass, that in the place where it was said unto them, Ye are not my people; there shall they be called the children of the living God.' (Rom. 9.25–6). What did those strange words mean? Later she read 'But Israel, following the law of righteousness, failed to reach the goal of righteousness' (Rom. 9.31). No problem there! It was just what the Koran said of the Jews. But then there followed: 'For Christ means the end of the struggle for righteousness by the law for everyone who believes in him' (Rom. 10.4).

Christ the end of the struggle? Could it be? Then she read on: 'For the secret is near to you, in your own heart, in your own mouth . . . If you openly admit by your own mouth that Jesus Christ is Lord, and if you believe in your own heart that God raised him from the dead, you will be saved' (Rom. 10.8–9).

Now the clash was clear. Either the Koran was right or the Bible was right. The Koran taught that Jesus didn't die on the cross but was taken up to heaven by God, that a substitute was put on the cross. Jesus would some day return for forty years of glory, and then die. There wasn't much agreement between the two accounts!

Then Bilquis started to dream. The first dream was about John the Baptist, and helped her later as she sought Christian initiation. The second was more mysterious. It was about a perfume salesman bringing her a golden jar. His perfume glimmered like liquid crystal. He placed the jar by her bedside. 'This will spread throughout the world.' She woke up to find her Bible in the place where the jar had been in the dream. Later as she walked in her garden, she had a strange sense of the fragrance of God. It wasn't flowers, it was different, far more beautiful. (Others, too, have told me of this experience. It happened to an aunt of my wife's in church one day.) Eventually some missionaries interpreted the dream: 'Thanks be to God who leads us, wherever we are, on Christ's triumphant way, and makes our knowledge of him spread throughout the

94

world like a fragrant perfume!' (2 Cor. 2.14).

Very soon Bilquis was a professing, baptized Christian. She faced much hostility for her new-found faith, and eventually left Pakistan to live in the U.S.A. Her conversion is another testimony to the power of Scripture.

For my own part, some fifteen years ago I was much troubled over the question of ordination. I prayed for nearly a year without receiving any clear guidance. Finally, in some desperation, I prayed, 'Lord, if you want me to be ordained, please make it very clear'. A fortnight or so later, I was on a parish holiday, and undergoing a sudden and deep emotional crisis. One Saturday evening, I spent a long time in prayer. God seemed to indicate both that he wanted me to give up any interest in a girl I had just fallen very deeply for (this was just as well as I was causing similar turmoil in her as she had just got engaged), and furthermore that he wanted me to give up the schoolmastering career, of which I was very fond, and to serve him full time. He also seemed to direct me to read Psalm 143; verse 8 in particular seemed significant. 'Show me thy loving kindness in the morning' became my prayer.

In the morning, still shaken and somewhat sceptical, I went to church. The then Rector of St Aldate's, Canon Keith de Berry, was preaching. I settled back to hear his interesting but somewhat predictable evangelistic sermon. When we sang Psalm 143, I sensed something strange was happening. When he preached on the transfiguration, I was listening to every word. Suddenly he said, 'When Jesus came down from the mountain, he faced a hard choice. Humanly speaking, he could have gone back to Galilee as a fairly successful minor prophet, or he could go on to Jerusalem and do what his Father wanted – something far harder. And', he continued 'there are some of you here this morning who have been Christians for quite a while, whom God is calling to make that harder choice . . .'

I didn't hear any more. The Word of God had broken my resistance. Reluctantly I set out on the trail towards ordination!

It would, of course, be wrong to suggest that Scripture's principal use is for guidance, or even for conversion. But when we experience its power in these ways, we are better able to meditate upon its words, and more willing to apply it to the whole of our lives. Scripture is our basic food and sustenance. Here are just a few verses which illustrate this great theme:

'How can a young man keep his way pure? By guarding it according to thy word.'

'I will delight in thy statutes; I will not forget thy word.'

'Open my eyes, that I may behold wondrous things out of thy law.'

'My soul melts for sorrow; strengthen me according to thy word!'

'How sweet are thy words to my taste.'

'Thy word is a lamp to my feet and a light to my path.' Ps. 119, verses 9, 16, 18, 28, 103, 105).

'Take the helmet of salvation, and the sword of the Spirit, which is the Word of God.' (Eph. 6.17).

'Let the word of Christ dwell in your richly.' (Col. 3.16).

'But as for you, continue in what you have learnt . . . from childhood you have been acquainted with the sacred writings which are able to instruct you for salvation through faith in Christ Jesus. All Scripture is inspired by God and profitable for teaching, for reproof, for correction, and for training in righteousness, that the man of God may be complete, equipped for every good work' (2 Tim. 3.14–17).

These are the very basic claims of Scripture, borne out in the experience of many. We all need the Scriptures for spiritual growth. Invariably when people seek help who are finding faith difficult or prayers lacking, it seems that two vital ingredients are missing – Bible reading and prayer.

Far too few churches teach these absolute necessities; even fewer give much idea of how to work at them for study. Basic Scripture reading needs order and explanation. Beginners need explanatory notes,[2] partly for instruction, and partly to provide a basic pattern to cover a wide range of Scripture. After that, it is good to read through an entire book to start getting the broad sweep of the writer's message. Simple commentaries – and there are some excellent ones[3] written with this need in mind – bring the Scriptures alive and deepen knowledge. Hard Bible study writes God's truths into our hearts in a practical way.

Church groups usually find the quality of their fellowship improves if their discussions have a scriptural basis. (This needs good leadership, otherwise the discussion degenerates into anecdotes, 'blessed thoughts', and arguments. The group will more readily discuss the existence of angels than how to share their faith with their workmates.) It helps if different church groups are studying the same things. One year, our St Matthew's fellowship groups did a course called 'Expressing his Life'.[4] This required a certain amount of homework, often best done in pairs, and made the participants think biblically and practically about their faith.

The text of the course gives lots of biblical references to help us find the basis for our answers, and lots of space to write down our own thoughts. The effect of the study was beneficial. It healed some divisions between people, and seemed to bring a unity and cohesion into the groups.

A church which, say, devoted Lent to studying the Epistle to the Ephesians would, by the time it had finished, have had a hard look at its doctrine (especially the question of sin, new rebirth, and reconciliation (Chapter 2), and the importance of the church), structure (the whole question of every member ministry, church growth, and individual's gifts and ministries (Chapter 4)), ethics (Chapter 5), family life (Chapters 5 and 6), and spiritual warfare (Chapter 6).

A church which is about to mount a stewardship campaign would be well advised to look first at the biblical basis of giving, both internally, and to other causes. They might then find themselves following the biblical example of a Bristol church which, when faced with financial crisis, started to give away ten per cent of what they received. A few years later, they were giving away what many churches would have regarded as a remarkable total income.

Preaching, too, is much improved when it is thoroughly biblically based. The Oxford Partners in Mission report had some trenchant things to say about sermons which had no basis in the readings at the service. They criticized much vague preaching on secondary issues. My own brief experience of visiting other churches, when on holiday or between jobs, seems to confirm this. Preaching today is seldom based on expounding the Bible (though the readings may well be used as a peg to hang ideas upon), and this seldom leaves the listener with any clear application of Scripture to his own life.

As a fairly secular society, we not surprisingly don't pay much attention to the Scriptures. King Jehoiakim (Jer. 36) disliked what was read by Baruch from Jeremiah's scroll. He sliced up the scroll with a penknife, and deposited the pieces in a burning grate. This didn't stop them coming true, or Jeremiah rewriting them (at greater length!). But Jehoiakim's contempt for the Word of God is repeated in every generation.

What would Amos and Hosea say to the western indifference to the needs of the third world? While they might commend the labours of missions and aid agencies, they would surely be scathing in their denunciation of our governments on this issue.

Our general morality is now quite independent of the Sermon on the Mount. Even our attitude to conservation shows little concern for the welfare of the creatures over whom we have dominion! (Gen. 1.28). The general stampede towards Sunday trading and sport shows little desire to worship God.

All of this is hardly surprising. We cannot really expect a largely unbelieving nation to submit, to its apparent inconvenience and disadvantage, to biblical standards. We might expect things to be better in the Church. But current church life has little biblical basis. Apart from the commendable centrality of the Eucharist in many of our churches (Luke 22.14–20; 1 Cor. 11.23–9), our worship suffers greatly from being comfortable and undisturbing. There is little lay participation; most clergy still do almost everything in the service themselves, and any idea of people coming prepared actively to participate (1 Cor. 14.26) would be regarded as a recipe for a disastrous babel. Baptism, despite the clear contrary teaching given in 1 Corinthians 10.1–5, is often held to be the sole required evidence for salvation. Churches pay lip-service to evangelism – accepting the fact that outsiders need to be converted, but with little will or ability to tackle the problem – but ignore the uncomfortable fact that many of their regular worshippers may be showing few signs of 'growing up to salvation'. Clergy are permitted to deny many of the scriptural fundamentals of the faith and to remain in office. Hardly surprisingly, many churches have dwindling congregations. God's judgement seems to be sifting us, testing our work and seeing what will stand.

> 'According to the grace of God given to me, like a skilled master builder I laid a foundation, and another man is building upon it. Let each man take care how he builds upon it. For no other foundation can any one lay than that which is laid, which is Jesus Christ. Now if any one builds on the foundation with gold, silver, precious stones, wood, hay, straw –

each man's work will become manifest; for the Day will disclose it, because it will be revealed with fire, and the fire will test what sort of work each one has done' (1 Cor. 3.10–13).

What sort of foundation are we building upon? Asking hard questions like that brought Graham Pulkingham, former rector of the Church of the Redeemer, Houston, to the edge of despair, and then face to face with God in a new and vital way.

There are of course signs of hope. The second Vatican Council unleashed something of a spring time in the Roman Catholic Church, and the worldwide Renewal movement has brought a fresh desire for unity, and a fresh experience of God, to many Christians of all denominations. One mark of these renewal experiences has been the reading of Scripture. Like the Ethiopian eunuch, people are starting to read – and to ask 'What does this mean?' Many, like me, have discovered that their old, rather cavalier attitude to Scripture has been replaced by a new submission to its teachings. When I started to discover that unusual things recorded in the New Testament still happened today – direct guidance, like the 'fleece' which set David Wilkerson off on the road to helping the drug addicts in New York (as recorded in *The Cross and the Switchblade*), healing, deliverance, prophecy – my faith in Scripture returned. When I began to discover that people were sometimes helped far more by a few clear applications of Scripture and prayer than by hours of listening and good advice, and that particular verses of Scripture could shed amazing light into dark corners, my intellectual resistance crumbled. Not yet a fundamentalist, I nevertheless felt a bit like Peter: 'Lord to whom shall we go? You have the words of eternal life' (John 6.68).

Those words now are primarily the words of Scripture.

NOTES

1   A useful compilation of Scripture reading.

2   Such as those published by the Scripture Union or the Bible Reading Fellowship; or *Every Day with Jesus*.

3   Especially 'The Bible Speaks Today' (IVP), a series of commentaries on specific Bible books, e.g. *God's New Society*, John Stott on Ephesians.

4   Published by Celebration Publishing.

11 *Prayer*

When parish visiting, one gets asked many fairly irrelevant questions; a few loaded ones about church policy, previous clergy, other parishioners and the like; and occasionally a really helpful one like 'Rector, how does one pray?' or, 'What does real commitment involve?'

Jesus was frequently questioned by opponents, hearers and disciples alike. Often the questions were hostile: 'Is it right to pay taxes to Caesar?' 'Is it lawful to heal on the Sabbath Day?' Sometimes they were naive: 'What does this parable mean?' But occasionally he, too, received a really helpful question. One such was: 'Lord teach us to pray, as John taught his disciples' (Luke 11.1).

Prayer – alone, in a small group, or in church – is a key part of 'growing up to salvation' (1 Pet. 2.2). Without prayer, we can scarcely enter the L-shaped field; without prayer we shall certainly fail to grow. Peter continues in verse 4: 'Come to him . . . and like living stones be yourselves built into a spiritual house, to be a holy priesthood, to offer spiritual sacrifices acceptable to God through Jesus Christ.'

We can scarcely expect to be part of a spiritual house, part of a holy priesthood, let alone offer spiritual sacrifices acceptable to God, unless prayer (and worship) are the nerve centre of our Christian practice and faith.

Jesus responded to the disciples' question with a version of what we know as the Lord's Prayer, and with the rather difficult parable about the friend who called at midnight asking for bread. The rest of his teaching (as recorded in the Gospels) was either by example or in a number of penetrating sentences which occur throughout his teaching.

It was his example of prayer which provoked the disciples' question. Earlier in the same Gospel (Luke 5.16), we read that 'he withdrew into the wilderness and prayed'. A more literal translation would be, 'He was retiring in the deserts and praying', which strongly suggests a habit of prayer running through days or even weeks. Pressed by the needs of the people, and the endless opportunities for preaching and ministry, he nevertheless made prayer a clear priority.

There were four special occasions from which Peter, especially, must have learnt much. The first was after the amazing Sabbath Day's ministry in Capernaum which we have already discussed (ch. 1). The second was when Jesus spent a night in prayer before choosing the twelve apostles (Luke 6.12). The result was surprising – a tax collector, a freedom fighter, a gloomy doubter, one who would betray him, and eight others, made up a motley band who would form the basis of the team which Jesus would train and Peter would lead, to shake the religious foundations of the world.

The third occasion was when Jesus took Peter, James and John up a mountain to pray (Luke 9.28). Luke is careful to record that it was while Jesus was praying that 'his countenance was altered and his raiment became dazzling white'. Prayer brought Jesus, already wonderfully close to God, into a new and even deeper experience.

The final occasion was in the Garden of Gethsemane. Here was fought the greatest battle in prayer which has ever taken place (Luke 22.39–46). Jesus knew what lay ahead if he stayed near Jerusalem. He knew that he could easily escape, but he had to be sure of his Father's will. His life had often been in danger, but God had protected him, allowing him to slip through hostile crowds. Was now the appointed hour? By his actions, and in particular in the institution of the Last Supper, Jesus had already declared that the end was at hand. Now he needed confirmation and strength: 'Not my will, but thine . . .'

He rose comforted, strengthened by an angel, spiritually ready to face the appalling pain of the final day. The disciples, already close to exhaustion, had fallen asleep. They, too, would have their prayer battles in the years ahead. Peter at least seemed to learn from the experience. In his first epistle there is a strong link between glory and suffering – a link surely forged in the prayer experiences of the Mount of Transfiguration and the Garden of Gethsemane. (see, e.g., 1.3–9; 4.13–15; 5.1).

Jesus assumed that people would pray regularly. His quarrel with the Pharisees was not the regularity but the ostentation of their prayers. He taught his disciples to go into a quiet room, and unseen to pray to their heavenly Father. Their prayer life, like an iceberg, was to be largely invisible. But there was never any question of it being an optional extra. 'When you pray . . .' (Matt. 6.5).

For beginners and more experienced Christians alike, there are two main problems: how to create time, and how to use the time. Everyone's lifestyle is different, but the creation of time to pray is an absolute necessity. One has only to read the biographies of effective Christian workers, of all traditions, to discover what a major part of their time was spent in prayer. We need once and for all to silence Satan's insidious accusation that the time we spend in prayer could better be spent in all manner of useful 'Christian' activity. One small discovery that I quickly made was that a good period of prayer before sermon preparation invariably meant that the whole job was completed far quicker than if I immediately sat down to write.

Many of us need a simple prayer pattern – indeed, that is the proper and intended use of the Lord's Prayer.

Praise is a good way of beginning. It is a way of coming into God's presence. At its simplest, it is thanking God for who he is. Jesus used this kind of prayer after the return of the seventy (Luke 10.21): 'In that same hour he rejoiced in the Holy Spirit and said "I thank thee, Father, Lord of heaven and earth that thou hast hidden these things from the wise and understanding and revealed them to babes; yea, Father, for such was thy gracious will".'

Many people find that their daily Bible reading leads them naturally into praise. Praise, or adoration, does not require a lot of words. When lovers meet, silence can be deeply meaningful. Indeed it is generally a sign of an insecure relationship if lots of verbal expressions of love are required. Jesus, in the Sermon on the Mount, and elsewhere in the Gospels commends restraint in speech.

We need to learn to be quiet before God.

'God is in heaven and you are on earth, so let your words be few', writes Ecclesiastes with characteristic pithiness (Eccl. 5.2 NIV).

'For God alone my soul waits in silence' (Ps. 62.5), remarks the Psalmist.

There is a long and honourable tradition of Christian meditation. Books like Richard Foster's *Celebration of Discipline* are helpful on how to learn some of the techniques. We must not be frightened of learning new methods. They can give our prayer life a framework from which we can move out into spontaneity and freedom.

Archbishop Anthony Bloom, in *School for Prayer*, tells a delightful story of how in his younger days an old lady sought his advice about prayer. She began, encouragingly, by telling him that she had been asking reputed experts for years about prayer without receiving any help! She suggested that he, as a young man, probably knew nothing, but he might by chance blunder out a helpful answer.

Thus encouraged, he advised her to straighten her room after breakfast, then to look around it and to appreciate it, and then to sit quietly for a quarter of an hour – knitting before the face of God. She was to say no prayers, just to sit quietly.

Some time later she came back to see him and said, 'You know, it works!' She had learnt to appreciate her room, had experienced fifteen minutes of real peace, and in the silence she began to feel the presence of God: 'All of a sudden I perceived that the silence was a presence. At the heart of the silence there was Him who is all stillness, all peace, all poise.'

We could all profit from the old lady's experience and realize that, in quietness, our souls will find rest, and that as we find rest, God will find us. In one busy pre-Christmas period, I led our church prayer group in quiet listening instead of our usual study and intercession. Everyone seemed delighted. There was a cool glow on their faces as some of their tiredness drained away. I, too, despite the apparent strain of leading, found the time enormously helpful.

The house of healing at Crowhurst in Kent teaches a special prayer of relaxation which involves relaxing the body, by sitting properly in a certain way, then relaxing the mind, by thinking back over some happy memory, and finally relaxing the spirit by meditating upon God's love. I've often used this prayer with tense and depressed people. Frequently they've fallen into a deep sleep in my study and woken up much later, considerably refreshed.

At the very least we should begin our prayer time by carefully and slowly reading a few verses of the Bible. This will direct our thoughts away from ourselves and out to God and his world. One Christmas a relative asked me to make some tape recordings of Scripture for use in his car. I found the effect of reading Scripture continuously for up to an hour at a time a very exciting experience. Inevitably one uses one's imagination far more than usual, and I found myself being thrilled as I noticed new phrases in well-known stories.

Confession is the next fundamental component of prayer. Some feel that this needs to come first, but the problem of this is that it means that our prayer time begins with us and our failings and not with God and His greatness.

Jesus frequently stressed the need when praying to seek the forgiveness of God and to forgive others (Matt. 6.12, 14; Mark 11.25, etc.). The parable of the Pharisee and the Publican (Luke 18.10–14) makes a sharp contrast between the unacceptable self-righteousness of the Pharisee and the simple confession of the Publican. We have already seen (ch.5) that both those aspects of forgiveness are essential to effective prayer.

Sometimes Christians declare that in their redeemed and victorious state they feel no need to confess anything. A friend once told me that he hadn't sinned for two days – thereby breaking his record I rather think! Watchman Nee has an interesting comment on this. 'No single deed of any Christian is originally white. Often we may have been outwardly kind to others but were inwardly resentful. Often we have been patient about someone only to go home and moan about him. Even after doing some righteous deed, we still need the cleansing of the blood.' The night that I first read this I had been chairing a PCC meeting where one member had been very trying. I had been feeling quite proud of my patience and was having a good moan about his conduct! I saw that my prayers needed to begin with asking for God's forgiveness for this wrong attitude.

Thanksgiving ought to be the easiest part of our prayer time. Even the smallest child and the newest Christian can usually find plenty to thank God for. God wants us to be grateful for his love and help, just as parents appreciate gratitude from their children.

There are two extreme and opposite reactions to such a statement. The cynic says, 'Why does God need our praises?' C.S. Lewis in *Reflections on the Psalms* has some apposite comments on this. The main point is not that God needs our praise, but rather that praise is a natural and spontaneous reaction to his goodness. It releases our souls to new heights and is one way in which we experience God's presence. This is equally true when we are alone or in the midst of some great congregation.

The opposite reaction is to quote 1 Thessalonians 5.18: 'Give thanks in all circumstances; for this is the will of God in Christ

Jesus for you' (or Colossians 3.17). This leads to the 'Praise-the-Lord-I've-broken-my-leg' syndrome, which is intellectually ridiculous and contrary to the balance of Scripture. Jesus himself did not praise in all situations – he wept over Jerusalem and he wept when he heard of Lazarus's death. He was angered by cynical questions, unbelief, and even the disciples' stupidity. Emphatically there were many times when he was much more the 'man of sorrows' than the man of praise. We can, of course, thank God after some misfortune for the fact that his presence is still with us and for what we can learn from the mistake or the accident.

The prayer of thanksgiving should be the simple response from our grateful hearts for God's love and provision. Like other forms of prayer, it needs practice and imagination – we can easily let it become stale and stereotyped. Incidentally, one of the many advantages of group prayer is that it is fascinating and instructive to learn from other people's prayers and to discover what makes them grateful. (In one prayer group, a certain member's praises were always prefaced with a great wail about the cobwebs in his life. At last another member could stand it no longer, and convulsed the group by thanking God aloud that He would 'kill the spider' in our friend's prayer life!)

Jesus also taught his disciples a great deal about intercession (asking). The parable of the 'friend at midnight' which was the second part of Jesus' answer to the disciples' question on prayer leads up to a great climax. 'If you then, who are evil, know how to give good gifts to your children, how much more will the heavenly Father give the Holy Spirit to those who ask him! (Luke 11.13)

The implication is clear – God our Father wants to bless us by answering our prayers in ways that are spiritually beneficial and appropriate. Jesus has two key phrases about this sort of prayer: 'abiding in me' and 'asking in my name' (see John 14—16). These are the keys to effective intercession either for individuals or for a group or for a church. We are not abiding in Christ unless we are spending time in quiet prayer and in trying to discover his will for the particular situation. If we are abiding in Christ, our actual intercession may be very brief. I have often marvelled at the brevity of Fred Smith's prayers for the sick, yet with the number of people who seek his prayers there is no way that he could spend long with any individual. I am sure the secret of this effectiveness is the time he spends alone with Christ far away from his public ministry.

A friend of mine, Julian, tells how he was praying late one night for the conversion of a friend. This is one of the hardest sorts of intercessory prayer. So many different factors are involved, chiefly that strange mixture of the timing of God's call and the free response of another human being. While Julian was praying, he had a clear sense of God saying, 'Go to bed, I've heard your prayer'. When he next met his friend, he discovered that he had become a Christian that very night!

The second key phrase is 'asking in my name'. The elderly clergyman I mentioned in chapter 1 of this book used to illustrate this by recounting how he had once been the guest of an American millionaire. The millionaire sent him off to visit America with an open cheque book signed with his own signature. At first he was embarrassed by this and didn't know what to do or where to stay. Then he realized that, as the millionaire's guest, he must go to the sort of places where he would stay. He was, after all, acting in his name. From then he had a marvellous holiday!

If we approach prayers by first thinking, 'Can I really ask this in Jesus' name?' or, 'Will this glorify his name?' we shall make fewer ridiculous requests. James' and John's mother (Matt. 20.20–3) would not have asked such a presumptuous favour if she had stopped to think if she could really ask this in the name of Jesus. His signature could hardly be written on such a selfish prayer request.

Sometimes we have courage to ask only for small things, and God uses this to encourage us to be bolder.

A man told me how he prayed for his next door neighbour's conversion. Yet there seemed to be no progress. Then God seemed to say, 'Pray for something smaller which you can believe will happen'. So he prayed to get into conversation with him. The next day they talked for the first time over the garden fence. Then he prayed that the conversations would be more significant, and immediately his neighbour asked him where he took his family off each Sunday morning. Things progressed gradually until his neighbour reached a point of faith!

It is a sad fact that when apparently real disciples tell one that 'it isn't working' and 'that they're about to give up', it is invariably their prayer life (or lack of it) which is the cause. A tree cannot spread itself properly without deep and wide roots, and a Christian will never grow without an ever-increasing prayer experience.

For some, the key to a renewed prayer life has been receiving the gift of praying in tongues (1 Cor. 12.10, etc). Sometimes new Christians experience this gift (Acts 19.6), and in some churches they are taught to expect it as a sign of the reality of the Holy Spirit's presence. There are undoubted dangers in exaggerating the importance of this gift – Jesus, as far as we know, never used it, and Paul wrote little about it. But equally it is foolish to deny people another potential channel for God's grace in their lives. Many people, myself included, find the gift especially helpful when ministering to the sick; others, both experienced and recent disciples, find it brings a freshness into their prayer life which otherwise seems to be lacking.

Praying alone is the most vital means of communication with God. Here, we are refreshed spiritually and physically; here, we often experience a most glorious sense of God's presence. This can come in a deep sense of peace, or in a sudden quickening of our whole body as 'our hearts burn within us' as we sense some directive from the Lord; in physical refreshment as we meditate quietly; in paeans of verbal praise or even tears as we pour out our gratitude to God.

Sometimes, however, God seems absent from our prayer room. We feel tired, dry, despairing and inclined to give up. It is at times like these, which frequently occur just after some spiritual high point or great spiritual battle, that we most need to persist.

Learning to trust God in times of his apparent absence is one of the necessary experiences of growing. The Psalmist in the desert (Ps. 84.6) knew this when he wrote, 'going through the vale of misery – they use it for a well'. A hibernating butterfly has to settle down to survive the winter without any food, yet when it awakes the following spring it has reached a new maturity and is ready to procreate the species. A child has to learn that it can survive, and even profit from the absence of its parents. Gradually these absences increase as the child grows towards maturity.

God seems to build into his servants a wide variety of experiences – times of great closeness and times of virtual absence. Very young Christians are often granted amazing answers to prayers. These encourage them out of the shadow of the woods into the centre of the L-shaped field. Later in life, they look back in wonder at these early experiences, but at the same time they realize they have reached a more mature and more secure faith. Churches experiencing renewal seem to have something of the same sort of experience. David Watson told how, in the early days of their renewal experiences at York, they had many examples of physical healing, whereas latterly there had been far fewer.

Important as solitary prayer undoubtedly is, it is not the only way of growth. We shall not learn much about being 'living stones in God's temple' if our experiences are entirely solitary. Praying with others is where we are most likely to meet the power of God. It is also a vital learning experience. Jesus taught his disciples by example. So did Paul, and many other masters of prayer throughout Christian history. As we hear others pray aloud, we learn from their spirituality, from their faith, their use of Scripture, etc.

Jesus is not recorded as having taught much about group prayer. Apart from the famous quotation (Matt. 18.19) – 'Again I say to you, if two of you agree on earth about anything they ask, it will be done for them by my Father in heaven. For where two or three are gathered in my name, there I am in the midst of them' – there is nothing else. This saying of Jesus stresses the need for agreement and unity. Indeed, the prayer comes in the context of going, in as loving a way as possible, to rebuke an erring brother. Often disunity and disharmony have to be confessed, before the holy agreement required by Jesus can be reached. I found a Christian colleague difficult for several years. (He, too, found me equally difficult!) But we faced this, worked through it, and once before a mission spent a memorable evening in prayer. That night, we seemed to reach a unity of purpose, a harmony of mind, and an expectancy of faith, which I have seldom experienced since. The mission that followed was in many ways the most remarkable that I can remember.

Jesus sent his disciples out in pairs (Mark 6.7). Presumably, they jointly prayed for the sick, preached and cast out demons. Most ministry of this sort is best done in pairs, or in a small group. It is a wonderful learning experience to pray alongside a more experienced Christian worker. Humbling, too, for the experienced man to find that God invariably gives unexpected insights to the apparently less able partner. The learning process in the Christian life is never completed. We are always 'growing up to salvation' as long as we are alive.

(Perhaps we should stress at this stage that salvation has a past, present and future tense. Our salvation is secured in the past by Jesus, it is experienced in the present as we know something of God's presence in our daily lives, and it will be completed in the future when we are 'transported from one degree of glory into another'.)

Even if Jesus isn't recorded as having taught the disciples to pray in groups, it quickly became a vital part of the experience of the apostolic Church. Immediately after the ascension (Acts 1.14) the Apostles gathered for prayer. They were joined by Mary, the faithful band of women who had ministered to Jesus, and his brothers.

The brothers included James, soon to become one of the leaders of the whole Church (Acts 15), now a witness to the resurrection (1 Cor. 15.7) and a very recent convert. James would have known something of private prayer from standard Jewish practice, but it is unlikely that he had ever prayed in a group.

For most new converts the experience of group prayer is both novel and slightly alarming. Yet this is an essential part of learning and growth. For those of us in such situations who are naturally tongue-tied, I would make a number of suggestions. Prepare a simple thank-you prayer, or ask God to place one person's needs on your heart so that you can pray for them. Sometimes groups, especially if they are new to such prayer, pray round in a circle. This simple technique at least removes the embarrassment of when to pray! Very soon such aids can be left behind, and the group will discover its own prayer dynamic. If praying aloud becomes a real problem, it can usually be overcome by seeking out one friend and just praying together in a pair.

I am certain that group prayer is important, and all of us need to learn to participate. Then, as the Holy Spirit leads us, we may also experience the gifts of the Spirit (1 Cor. 12). I've known very young disciples given pictures or Bible verses which have been important for the whole group.

One of the most memorable apostolic prayer meetings is recorded in Acts 4.23–31. The Apostles had been arrested, threatened, and reluctantly released. They had been warned not to speak, preach or pray in the name of Jesus. What was their response? To give up? To draw back? Quite the reverse! Powerfully and confidently, they prayed for more healing (and it was healing that had got them into trouble!), for more boldness (and they had already displayed great boldness in their public ministry), and for more signs and wonders to confirm their words. They also gently reminded God of some scripture which was relevant to the situation, and left the matter in his hands. God's answer was to enter the room in a marvellous way and fill them again with his Holy Spirit. These men, already deep in the experiences of the Spirit, prayed for and received more of God's power. Would that we who are so easily content with spiritual crumbs had this sort of hunger!

Sometimes during missions, churches seem to experience something like this. Many times I have heard St Aldate's teams return and testify to final evenings where great freedom, and a real sense of God's sovereign power had been experienced. People had been suddenly converted, healed, or set free from various sorts of bondage, with little or no actual ministry. Often such evenings would have been preceded by great battles in prayer as the team fought against apparent indifference in the area and their own very real sense of failure.

Reading Colin Urquhart's book *Faith for the Future* makes me realize how feeble most prayer meetings are, and how little we experience of God's presence and holiness. It is as though, to revert to the L-shaped field, we cling to the shadows when we pray and never come out into the sunlight.

There are many reasons for this, but fear, rebellion and hardness of heart seem key factors. We are afraid of real experience – hence the reaction of church groups to anything new. We are often in a state of rebellion, and until there is repentance the group cannot move forwards. Our hearts are hard, we dislike hearing of spiritual matters, and we don't really care about the dryness of ourselves, our group, and our church. Ezekiel 36.26 (often read at confirmation services) brings us the promise of a new heart – a heart of flesh to replace the heart of stone – which is part of the new experience of God as we enter his Kingdom. The problem for so many of us is that this new heart quickly becomes petrified as we seek to keep control of our own lives and to keep the Spirit out.

A third memorable apostolic prayer meeting is recorded in Acts 12. Peter had been arrested and was in great danger of being executed (as James the brother of John had been by Herod). The Church gathered for earnest prayer. So earnest that when Peter was released and interrupted their prayers with his loud knocking, they assumed that it was a vision! Even they couldn't believe that God had answered their prayers so quickly and so dramatically.

I personally know that one friend of mine felt led to pray for me with great intensity precisely at the time when I was experiencing some real physical danger. The next evening, a church fellowship group were praying for me, which was just as well, as with the help of a sturdy parishioner and two other unlikely allies, I was beating a rapid retreat from a house, pursued by an armed man! Another friend recalls how when he was in the navy he experienced a time of great danger in a typhoon. When he returned to his Scottish church, he was surprised to learn that at the time an old lady had roused her household to pray for him with the words, 'Pray for Edward, he is in great danger.'

Such stories are very numerous. It seems that part of Christian sensitivity to the Holy Spirit is learning to listen so that we can intercede for the right people at the right time.

The fourth recorded prayer meeting in Acts took place in Antioch (Acts 13.1–3). Here, after worship and a time of fasting, the Holy Spirit communicated with the Church the devastating message that two leaders, Barnabas and Saul, were to be set aside, prayed for, and sent off. The effect on the Antioch church could have been disastrous. Who was to lead them? . . . We are not told much more about the church in Antioch; presumably it survived! But we do know of the amazing results of the Holy Spirit's directive. Paul's three missionary journeys established new bases for the Church all over the civilized world.

How did the Holy Spirit communicate with the Church? Possibly by a word from one of the Antioch prophets which was tested and confirmed by others in the leadership. Sadly there are few cases of God communicating as directly today with whole churches – still less with synods and councils. Imagine the effect of a diocesan conference, if an archdeacon announced that God's word was for both the bishops to leave and become missionaries!

One of the leaders of a church which I know well suffered from multiple sclerosis. He was a young man, and although the disease was in a relatively early stage, the outlook wasn't good. The whole church gathered for their normal Sunday service, but took time in the midst of it to pray for him and to anoint him with oil. He made a dramatic recovery. On that occasion there was tremendous preparation, unity, and a certain amount of expectancy. So often the corporate prayer life of a church is monotonous, boring and faithless. How can any new believer experience any growing up to salvation when the intercessions consist of a list of prayers for an unknown diocese, the current world problem, an impersonal list of sick people, and a commemoration of faithful departed? It is doubtless right to pray for all these things, but it is more important to get the church praying in faith for some clear objectives rather than in vague generalities.

I firmly believe that the prayers of the churches contributed to the relatively peaceful end of the Zimbabwe problem. I am sure that the prayers of the English churches at the time of the Dunkirk evacuation were heard (without which I, for one, wouldn't have been born!), and I believe that the prayers of the Church are vital in the pressing matter of nuclear disarmament.

But for the new disciple (and for older ones too) it may be more realistic and more effective to pray for the obvious needs of the local church. At the time of writing my church needs to pray specifically about a stewardship campaign, a new family service, and a Lent course. If we can pray unitedly about these three things, we shall begin to see God at work in our midst.

Finally, to revert to the importance of solitary prayer. D.L. Moody, the famous American evangelist of the last century, was in England. He was a young man, and his great work hadn't really begun. He was invited to preach in a big London church. In the morning, he sensed nothing memorable despite large numbers. In the evening, the whole atmosphere was different. The church was alive in the Spirit! Scores of people answered his call for commitment. The response was so great that he had to minister for several nights. This, humanly speaking, led to the salvation of thousands. Intrigued, he tried to find out what was the difference between morning and evening congregations.

Eventually he tracked down a bed-ridden woman whose sister came to the church. Every Sunday she would ask her sister about the services. Inevitably she would be given a monotonous and uneventful account. One Sunday the sister mentioned that a Mr Moody from America had preached. 'Ah!' said the bed-ridden one, 'I will have no lunch. I must pray'. She had once read an article by Mr Moody, and had prayed for *several years* for God to bring him to England to her church. Now her prayer had been answered, and things were going to happen! The results of that prayer were far-reaching for her church, and even more so for the world-wide church – a new spiritual giant was born.

How easy it would have been for that old lady to have lain back in bed saying, 'I am old, I am ill, I have grown up to salvation, there is nothing much more for me to do'. Indeed she produced her most effective spiritual work from her sick bed.

> Lord teach us how to pray aright
> with reverence and with fear.

12 *Fellowship*

A black South African pastor told of how he had discovered that Christian fellowship could cut right across social and racial barriers. He had been involved with radical student groups, and although still passionately concerned about the injustices in his country, was now seeking to work through the Church.

Driving along a road one day, he picked up a hitchhiker. As was his custom he began to share with his passenger the good news of the gospel. The man seemed unusually receptive, and professed conversion then and there. The pastor soon discovered why. The man was in deep trouble, and was on the run from the police for several robberies. However his profession of faith seemed genuine, and they kept in touch.

Not long afterwards the man was arrested, and his new Christian friend went to court on his behalf. He received a light sentence of just six months in prison. This entitled him to take part in an experiment, whereby some rich farmer would use him as a labourer for the six months instead of being kept in gaol.

The pastor had a very rich white friend who, when he heard the man's story, agreed to take on the prisoner he described. The day came for the scheme to start. White farmer and black pastor stood together at the prison gates. When the prisoner emerged, the farmer started back. 'I can't take him,' he protested. 'He's a thief. He's worked for me before!' The pastor thought quickly, and gently reminded the farmer of Onesimus and Philemon. Onesimus, before his conversion, had probably stolen from Philemon, but this didn't stop Paul from reminding him that they were brothers in Christ. The farmer repented of his attitude, and gladly took the man. Now he is actively involved both in promoting the scheme, and also in the much wider struggle for racial justice in South Africa. The Epistle to Philemon had opened his eyes.

By contrast, about five years ago Jane and I were picnicking by the River Gard in France. We met a very charming young German. He showed Jane the best part of the river to swim in, and settled down to talk to me. He told me how he had rejected the Church as a teenager in favour of revolutionary Marxism. He would have supported the Baader-Meinhoff gang of terrorists, but he regarded them as somewhat amateurish and not sufficiently political! He dismissed Christianity with a few sweeping references to the Epistle to Philemon. Far from regarding Paul as enlightened, he condemned him for accepting the prevailing system of slavery. Paul, for him, was an unimaginable bourgeois intellectual!

It is interesting to see how two intelligent people – the black pastor, who had rejected the revolutionary way, and the German Marxist – could make such different use of Paul's one-page letter.

'I appeal to you for my child, Onesimus . . .' Paul wrote (verse 10). Philemon, the slave owner, and Onesimus, one of his slaves, had become brothers in the Lord. Some years earlier Philemon had been converted through Paul's ministry (verse 19), and he had become a house church leader. (This responsibility he shared with a woman, Apphia, and Archippus who was bidden at the end of Colossians 'to fulfill the ministry which you have received in the Lord'. Leadership was evidently shared, and women played a full part.)

Philemon was a hospitable man (verse 7), he had entertained Paul, and Paul hoped to come to stay again (verse 22). He clearly used his house, and presumably his influential position, to promote the gospel.

Onesimus, by contrast, was a slave. Paul's letter hints, though not conclusively, that he was a thief (verse 18). He would probably have had to steal money in order to make his escape from Philemon's house, which was somewhere near Colossae in Greece. He made his way to Rome, where he somehow found the imprisoned Paul, and heard the good news of the gospel. Probably he had met Paul when he came to Philemon's house – Paul always took an interest in the whole household, and he would have preached to everyone including the slaves. Since by now Paul was in prison in Rome, Onesimus must have taken a considerable risk in seeking him out. After his conversion, Onesimus became Paul's servant and friend. Paul even makes a pun out of his name: 'Formerly he was useless to you, but now he is indeed useful (which is the meaning of the Greek word *onesimus*) to you and to me.'

Eventually, Paul sensed that he must send Onesimus back to Philemon, perhaps with a small group of Christians taking letters to the Colossian church. He wrote a careful covering letter to Philemon, reminding him that he owed his own spiritual life to Paul, and offering to pay for any damage that Onesimus had done. He begged Philemon to receive Onesimus back, not as a slave, but as a beloved brother.

This makes a remarkable contrast with a letter found in the Egyptian desert (c.AD 300) where an angry slave owner writes:

I commission you by this writ to go to the famous city of Alexandria and search for my slave about thirty-five years of age, whom you know. When you have found him you shall place him in custody, with authority to shut him up and whip him, and to lay complaint before the proper authorities against any persons who have harboured him, with a demand for satisfaction.'[1]

Paul expected Philemon to break one of the greatest barriers in the ancient world. He had written earlier to the Galatians (Gal. 3.28): 'There is neither Jew nor Greek, there is neither slave nor free, there is neither male nor female; for you are all one in Christ Jesus.' Philemon's house church with Apphia in co-leadership demonstrated part of that great declaration; now he was being asked to take things rather further. The church in his house would never quite be the same again.

There is a romantic theory that Onesimus was the first-century Christian who made the general collection of Paul's letters. About fifty years later, Ignatius, one of the early martyr bishops, was being taken from Antioch, his bishopric, to Rome for execution. As he went, he wrote many letters including one to the church in Ephesus. He has much to say about their remarkable bishop called Onesimus. Furthermore, Ignatius makes the same pun as Paul had done earlier about the man's name. Now it is virtually certain that Paul's letters were collected around this time and at Ephesus. But why has the little letter to Philemon survived – unless the collector had a personal interest in it? Is its survival Onesimus's personal testimony to the grace of God which had brought him from slavery to Christian leadership?

If Onesimus did become a bishop, it says much for the quality of fellowship in Philemon's house church. If a runaway slave could grow into a church leader, then barriers were really broken and growth experienced.

When someone is born anew, he also becomes part of the people of God. In the very chapter where Peter writes of the 'new birth' and 'growing up to salvation' he also states, 'Once you were no people; but now you are God's people' (1 Pet. 2.10). This can only happen if the new believer is integrated into the fellowship of the Church. If this doesn't happen, faith will wither, and another potential disciple will join the depressing list of those who claim to have committed themselves to Christ, but whose actual discipleship has been virtually non-existent.

What the new believer first needs is a special nurture or beginners' group, where he (or she) will be taught the fundamentals of the faith – prayer, Bible study, the doctrine of the cross, the evidence for the resurrection, experience of the Holy Spirit, the need to worship and to receive communion – and will experience fellowship with others at the beginning of their Christian journey. Often such groups nurture an impressive flowering of understanding and zeal.

I remember one particular girl to whom I had several times tried to explain the basics of the faith, with a total lack of success. Then she was truly converted and she joined a beginners' group. From then on, her understanding grew rapidly, and she soon became well integrated into another small group in the church.

That is the next step. After the nurture group, new disciples should be able to join a house group. Here they should be welcomed as bringing new life and new gifts to the group, and they should be able to spread their wings and put down secure roots.

The ideal house group provides a setting in which believers can get to know one another, pray for one another, serve one another, and learn to debate (and disagree!) about matters of real concern. It creates real friendships and a sharing of common interests amongst members. It should also aim to grow, and to divide!

I have seen house groups help fellow-members move house; cook regular meals for the sick and elderly; provide prayer and practical support for missionaries; support a church member with real psychological difficulties; provide baby sitters for a single parent; and do all manner of practical tasks. One group I know organized a collection to pay for turf for someone's garden, and then got down to the practical problem of laying a lawn.

As people begin to feel at home in the group, they will begin to share their real problems (and joys!). When this happens, effective prayers can be offered, and a solution looked for.

Membership of such groups is not necessarily easy. According to temperament, there is the temptation always to remain silent or else to use every opportunity to air one's particular hobby horse! Differences in attitude regarding spirituality or politics will quickly emerge. Some members may want to experiment in worship, and use the gifts of the Spirit, in a way that is threatening and unacceptable to others. In this area, praying for the sick, especially those present or their immediate families, has proved to be an acceptable way of opening up group prayer and ministry. Even the controversial gift of tongues can often be used without upsetting anyone!

Political differences, too, must be faced. Some may want to keep the group away from political issues and keep to the 'simple gospel'. Others may be sceptical of attempts to care for the underprivileged and may want to attempt to integrate the group's caring with the State network. These differences of outlook need to be explored, and a common mind sought.

Today the nuclear debate is bound to surface. It is vitally important that Christian groups should not avoid controversies of this sort. If the Church is ever to speak effectively, it will only happen because the matter has been thoroughly debated at group level. Some members may feel led to join an organization like CND. The Christian CND member will find some strange companions, and will need the support of his group. (Even if they don't agree with his stand, they should be glad to have Christian involvement in such organizations.)

How often should house groups meet? There is obviously no fixed rule about this. Experience has shown that they cease to be effective if they meet less frequently than once a fortnight, and a weekly meeting is ideal. (This will inevitably affect other existing church organizations which may be found to be superfluous.)

The group programme should include social events such as visits to films and concerts, and shared suppers. Not all meetings need to be of a 'religious' nature. The aim will be to encourage genuine friendships within the group which will greatly strengthen the fellowship. There should also be some open meetings to which unbelieving (or uninterested) husbands, wives and neighbours can be invited. These need not be overtly evangelistic, although evangelism and growth will be another aim of the group.

All group members should be encouraged to take a share in the leadership. With a little help, even the most inexperienced can introduce a summary of a tape (for instance of Gerald Priestland's radio series *Priestland's Progress*), lead a short Bible study, or a time of prayer. A more experienced leader may need to spend some time convincing a shy group member that he (or she) is capable; but the results will usually prove the time well spent.

Participating in leadership, even in this sheltered environment, helps faith to grow and helps the person to value the group even more. (They may also be less critical of the established leadership when they discover how difficult even Christian meetings can be!) Shared leadership will also prepare the group for its next stage – to divide and grow.

Many members will not like the idea. 'We've just got used to the idea of a group and now you want us to move on . . .!' But unless a group is encouraged to grow it will tend to become introverted, safe, and ultimately pretty dead. Once the group has more than a dozen regular members, it is large enough to divide. Obviously this must be done prayerfully with full consultation of both church leadership and group members.

Experience shows that the whole church will benefit from house groups. Many routine tasks, such as making coffee after church, can best be delegated to house groups. The security which the group provides should make its members more outward looking and welcoming to strangers. Visitors can be very sensitive to the atmosphere in a church. They sense very quickly whether or not it is a welcoming and caring fellowship. If it isn't they will probably leave, and either look elsewhere or stop looking for help from the church.

One very shy woman crept into the St Aldate's lunchtime service. She was looking for help but didn't like to ask. To her surprise, people spoke to her and seemed to take a genuine interest. Gradually she opened up about herself and her husband who was in prison. Very gently, her new friends showed how Jesus could meet her need, her worry, and her loneliness. She became a Christian. Diffidently, she shared her new experience with her husband, and was amazed to discover that he also had become a believer. They faced the future with renewed confidence. He got his old job back, and they began a life of service to the Master who had served them so well.

Where a church has some experience of fellowship, it becomes more capable of supporting those in real trouble. One couple gave themselves entirely to another family in deep trouble. For about two years, the wife, in particular, would go round to support, direct and encourage a very fragile household. Often it seemd as if their efforts would be wasted, as some new crisis threatened to shipwreck all the progress. But their self-service was rewarded (and of course, the Christian ideal of service expressed by Ignatius Loyola is 'to give and not to count the cost, to labour and not to ask for any reward save that of knowing that we do Thy will') and a family was saved from disaster. The original couple were greatly helped by other church families who acted as backups and prayer support, until gradually the burden of ministry shifted from them to the local church. Ultimately the family concerned moved from a sort of parasitic dependence into a mature faith where, despite a few crises, they were able to support and to give to others. They were certainly able to obey 1 Peter 2.9 and to tell others about 'him who called you out of darkness into his marvellous light'. Such ministry is very costly and cannot be undertaken unless the fellowship of the church is sufficiently strong to enable the burden to be shared.

Finance is another important, but often unrecognized, area of communal responsibility. A church that I know of has a fund to which all its members contribute. It is then used to help people, usually church members, who are in financial difficulty. It is administered by a small group of people specially chosen for the job. This shared responsibility has much to commend it; it relieves the rector from agonizing decisions over his small (in some cases microscopic) discretionary fund, and it also has a far wider application. Another way in which valuable help can be given is through interest-free loans which enable a young couple to buy a house which otherwise would have proved impossible.

It requires a good deal of grace and trust to give and receive in these sorts of ways. A church which manages this sort of practical fellowship should have few financial problems.

Once some sort of fellowship has been established within the local church, it will then be easier to recognize the needs and to share fellowship with the church overseas. Paul (see 2 Cor. 8; Phil. 4.14–20; Acts 11.27–30) was most anxious to set up this sort of international fellowship.

A reasonably active local church can do a remarkable amount if it catches a vision. In St Matthew's, through a single gift day, we were able to finance a medical missionary in Pakistan for a year. Over another two years, we supported a missionary family while they did their theological training. This was done by setting up a separate parish fund stewarded by two of the leaders of the church. In 1982, we became the centre for a relief trip to Poland. This grew out of a visit which one family had made to Gdansk a few years earlier. A close friendship was established (and sealed when Kasia, the mother of the Polish family, was dramatically healed of pleurisy through prayer). This led the senior member of the party to organize her own relief trip in the spring of 1982. The church became a warehouse – receiving basic food, medicine and clothing to a value of some £20,000 donated by people and churches over a wide area. Although this was only a drop in the ocean, the container-load of 'family' parcels was much appreciated in Gdansk.

Of course, such support is two-way. An outward-looking church gains immeasurably when it is visited by people from overseas who often bring a freshness and depth of faith that seems lacking at home. St Aldate's has many overseas links and a long tradition of generous giving. One year, rather imaginatively, they paid for the replanting of a forest in Haiti by TEAR fund. A number of their young people have gained much from one-year assignments abroad, and the steady stream of foreign visitors adds a richness to the experience and worship of the church.

But are we doing enough? The parable of the sheep and the goats (Matt. 25.31–46) ought to be a constant challenge against complacency. The gap between the affluence of the West and the poverty of many other countries continues to grow. What can we do to begin to put the Third World first? So many of us put up with dual standards. A white South African doctor came to England partly so that his son wouldn't be drafted into the Namibian border war. He complained bitterly of the poor medical facilities in Oxford as compared with those in his home country, while a missionary friend working in a black hospital in Zululand was bewailing the lack of the most basic drugs in her part of South Africa! Small wonder some Christians feel the need to identify with their underprivileged brethren in some sort of political action.

Most of us will have read the right books – like John Taylor's *Enough is Enough* or Ronald Sider's *Rich Christians in an Age of Hunger* – but we find it hard to know how to take the matter any further. George Hoffman, director of TEAR fund, has a telling phrase about Christians 'earning the right to speak'. As TEAR fund have built wells in Bangladesh, set up local industries, or built sewers in refugee camps, so they have found a steady hunger for the bread of life. As they have begun to serve their fellow humans, so they have gained new Christian brethren.

And what of the underprivileged in our own country? The church has a duty to help those with little hope and few prospects. I was once involved with setting up and managing a government-sponsored scheme for fifty unemployed teenagers. Sadly, I often felt under pressure from the church which owned the property where we were based, because the work wasn't 'overtly Christian'.

Perhaps some system of twinning parishes could be tried. A rich suburban parish could be twinned with a poor inner city parish. They could share resources, experiences and difficulties. Each would gain from the different vision of the other. Obviously there would be a danger of the rich patronizing the poor, but with sensitivity and tact this could be overcome. Speaking personally, I have gained immeasurably from brief periods of service in the poorer part of the country. At the very least, one's eyes are opened and one has a real sense of what it is like to live in the middle of a concrete jungle.

There are sadly many barriers to fellowship in most churches. 'Private' religion in probably the most insiduous of these. The Gospel according to 'private' religion says that solitary church-going is all that is required. Fellowship, and any talk of it, is a lot of nonsense. Furthermore, the church building and its services are sacrosanct, and any attempt to tamper with them is met with fierce opposition. (I had an elderly cousin who stopped going to church when her new vicar stood at the door of the church and attempted to shake her hand!)

Class and race also create barriers. Class consciousness perpetuates division, and makes people suspicious of one another. One of my friends in St Matthew's was very dubious when I arrived. What would a public school and Oxford graduate have

122

in common with a British Leyland worker? Yet gradually the barriers came down, as I visited his house regularly, and enjoyed watching football on TV (which with his family present was as full of comment and as loud as being at a match!). Eventually I prepared him for confirmation. After the confirmation service, another barrier was broken, when for the first time ever (after years of refusal) he called me John. Our friendship grew, and will, I hope, survive my departure. Although naturally uncertain about house groups, he has become an eloquent member of one of the church groups.

Part of the barrier is intellectual. Anglican services are in particular very 'wordy'. The new Alternative Service Book (of which I heartily approve) has so many pages and alternatives that someone not used to doing much reading is easily confused. Efforts to make services informal, and to involve lay people, have an intellectual appeal to certain types of people but discomfort others who need the safety of a set routine.

House groups have a tendency to become middle-class enclaves. Such people feel more at ease in one another's houses, talk more easily, and generally fit in. Nevertheless once this sort of barrier is broken – as it must be – the groups are greatly enriched by having a wide diversity of types of people within them.

At St Matthew's, we found a youth organization, the Boy's Brigade, a great help. With part of its emphasis on uniform and discipline, it appealed to the ordinary non-churchgoing family. Parents were able to contribute to its life by providing help at parties, football matches, rambles, jumble sales, etc. Through the BB, they gradually began to feel part of the church. An established BB group has infinitely more Christian potential in this respect than most other kinds of youth group.

The colour barrier is equally obvious in English churches. In south Oxford, there were many Asian Christian families – but they didn't come to our church. We had an excellent relationship with their pastor, but that was about as far as it got. In a church like St Aldate's, you will find people from all over the world. There appears to be a great mixing of the races. But as you talk to them, you find that almost all the non-whites are overseas students. Within a mile of St Aldate's, a black West Indian congregation meets for worship, and the Asians also meet together. This seems typical of the English scene. There is little fellowship which cuts across this barrier. How many coloured ordinands are there in the Church of England?

Differences of churchmanship cause less division now than in the past, although difficulties can still be formidable. Probably a more serious barrier is in the area of revelation and the supernatural. Christians from different traditions who share a common belief in the efficacy of prayer, the reality of the spiritual battle, the need for conversion and discipleship, will have much more to unite them than to divide them. I recently exorcized a house jointly with an Anglo-Catholic priest. We were completely at one in this action, recognizing a common enemy, and using common weapons. By way of contrast, my first theological college was very sceptical of any such beliefs. The final straw, for me, was when a senior member of staff preached a sermon saying in effect that intercessory prayer for specific things was a waste of time. I was so amazed that I tackled him in private, to make sure that I hadn't misunderstood him. He confirmed his views. I'm told that he has long since changed his attitude. But I'm afraid I didn't wait to find out . . .

All these barriers can be overcome with love and humility. As Paul writes (in the passage very appropriately used as the epistle for Church Unity Week): 'I beg you to lead a life worthy of the calling to which you have been called, with all lowliness and meekness, with patience, forbearing one another in love, eager to maintain the unity of the Spirit in the bond of peace . . .' (Eph. 4.1–3). Philemon, we believe, received Onesimus with love and humility. As a result Onesimus grew and flourished, and became 'useful' to the church universal.

So it should be with each new believer. If their first experience of fellowship is warm and welcoming, they will flourish. In due course, their gifts will be of use to the church and some of them will even be ready to lead the group they joined when it grows and divides. True fellowship is the best help for the individual who really wants to know what it means to be 'growing up to salvation'.

NOTE

1   Quoted by Michael Green in *Evangelism in the Early Church* (Hodder & Stoughton 1973), p.118.

13 *Suffering*

'Behold I see the heavens opened' (Acts 7.56).

Stephen, like Philip (see Chapter 9), was one of the seven deacons appointed by the early Church to sort out the dispute between the Greek and Jewish widows over the distribution of food and money. He is described, like Barnabas (Acts 11.24), as 'a man full of faith and of the Holy Spirit'.

After receiving the laying on of hands by the Apostles, he was also described as being full of grace and power. It is not clear whether the 'great signs and wonders' which accompanied his ministry (Acts 6.8) were a result of this apostolic commissioning or were already part of his experience.

He was also a fine speaker. Like Paul later, he was prepared to go into the synagogue and debate with the Jews. In those early days, a number of priests were converted (verse 7). These were probably saintly men of the ordinary order of priests (as opposed to the worldly and self-interested High Priests), a group which had included such humble seekers after truth as Zechariah, the father of John the Baptist. Doubtless these defections were noticed, and added to the tension of the debate.

It seems that at some stage Stephen expounded Jesus' recorded statement, 'Destroy this temple, and in three days I will raise it up' (Acts 6.14, see John 2.19). The Temple was a very sensitive issue, and Stephen's use of the Old Testament was somewhat unusual. He regarded favourably the wandering tabernacle in the wilderness, and seems to have considered the building of Solomon's great Temple as a retrograde step.

This was radical and subversive stuff. Even the church leaders hadn't entirely abandoned the Temple connection, and here was Stephen reducing its importance dramatically. He seems to have already caught a vision of fulfilling the Ascension Day command 'to go out into all the world', rather than staying in Jerusalem and waiting for the world to come there. Ironically it was his death, and the subsequent persecution of the Christians, which paved the way for the real spread of the gospel.

The Jewish listeners (especially as they were the 'freedmen' who had come to Jerusalem from afar) very likely sympathized with his arguments, but disliked his conclusions. This, together with the occasional 'sign' or 'wonder', must have made him a very trying opponent.

Eventually they'd had enough. It was not difficult to find a few false witnesses to twist his pretty dangerous words. Stephen was hauled before the Council, in a way that was very reminiscent of his Lord's appearance there. And those gazing at him saw the face of an angel. Not the mild, seraphic look of angels in medieval paintings, nor even the burning look of an avenging angel, but a look that told of inner inspiration. Clear bright eyes burned with fervour and with courage. Was it Saul of Tarsus who saw and remembered that look?

Stephen was allowed to make a very considerable speech. The customs of the Sanhedrin allowed and expected religious debate. The early part of the speech they would have found acceptable, and they would have agreed with Stephen's choice of critical moments in their history. It was the conclusion he drew, and his final challenge, which enraged them: 'You, leaders, have always resisted the Holy Spirit. You killed and persecuted all the prophets, and now you've killed the Righteous One – the Messiah.'

Enough is enough! The Jewish leaders began to seethe with anger. Stephen, as he grew steadily more inspired, saw a vision of God and told his hearers about it. It was too much, and judicial mayhem took place.

We cannot tell whether Stephen's death was the result of mob violence or judicial sentence. Possibly Pilate was back in Rome (the date was about AD 36), in which case this execution, like that of James, the brother of the Lord (in AD 61), would have been legal. More probably, Pilate had moved to Caesarea and could be relied upon to turn a blind eye. Stephen, like his Master, died with words of forgiveness for his executioners. The effects of his death were remarkable, and a new stage in the Church's mission started. Probably the greatest single effect was to prepare the way for the conversion of Saul of Tarsus.

Jesus warned his followers that persecution was almost inevitable, and his disciples have always had a difficult time. Over the last forty years, the Church has withstood persecution in many corners of the world. From Eastern Europe to China, from Iran to South Africa, in many parts of South America, it has been under attack. And, by and large, it is in these places that there has been growth. By contrast, in West Germany, where the

Church should have been more outspoken against Hitler, it has become weak. In East Germany, the Church has had to learn again what it means to stand for Christ in a hostile environment and it is quite strong. To be a Christian today in Eastern Europe is very costly. Only in Poland is the Church sufficiently large to be free, and there it has the delicate and difficult role of balancing the extreme freedoms sought by some* counter-revolutionaries and the just demands of the masses of her people. In many other parts of the Eastern bloc, to be a Christian is to be a social leper. Many professions, such as lecturing and teaching, are not open to Christians, and there is always the threat of a sudden clamp down. Evangelism is usually forbidden, and there are many other restrictions which may be enforced at any time.

There is also the difficult choice as to whether to belong to an 'underground' church where the worship is free but there is a constant state of turmoil and danger, or to a registered church which may be full of informers and fellow travellers.

The sufferings of Richard Wurmbrand, Pastor Vins, and the Siberian Seven are comparatively well known, but they are only the tip of the iceberg. One of the most moving stories in Wurmbrand's book *In God's Underground* describes how, when he was seriously ill in prison, he received an illicit gift of two lumps of sugar. He didn't eat the sugar, but passed it on to someone who was in a worse state. Again the sugar wasn't eaten. Apparently it lasted for some two years, passed from one prisoner to another, as a symbol of self-sacrifice and hope.

Recent evidence from China suggests that the Church there has withstood the persecution and the shocks of the first thirty years of communism remarkably well. Many leaders, like Watchman Nee, died in prison, but there are now tremendous signs of life. We in the comfortable West shall probably never know of the ingenuity and the courage of the saints who have kept the faith alive in that country.

A different sort of courage has been required of Christians in Uganda, South Africa, Northern Ireland, and parts of South America. Their faith was not illegal, and yet frequently they found themselves in collision with the government or popular opinion. The martyrdom of Archbishop Luwum, presumably for telling General Amin a few home truths, was but one of thousands in the period of terror in Uganda. The courage of that church, and its growth in the midst of suffering, will be one of the brightest pages of the Church's history this century.

Christians in many non-Christian countries are under great pressure. Conversions are deeply resented and evangelism is illegal. In Iran, the Church can expect little government protection, and it has suffered greatly since the Revolution.

In a different way, the discerning Christian in South Africa faces just as hard a task. Certainly the churches are awakening to the evils of *apartheid*. The Anglican Church, the first white church to speak out, has seen a remarkable revival which has followed its faithful and costly social witness. White and black face different dilemmas. For the white Christian it may be how far to go on the road of protest and civil disobedience; for the black it may be the harder question of how to avoid being sucked into revolution. Sometimes the Christian seems called to stand in the middle, pointing to the almost impossible way of reconciliation, and thereby earning the displeasure of both left and right.

This dilemma is repeated in much of South America, and in Northern Ireland, where ecumenical work has been slow and painstaking. The rewards are few, the occasional mutual forgiveness of Catholic and Protestant very wonderful, but the progress is painfully slow as each side uses a Christian label to support its particular brand of violence.

But all of this is fairly far removed from the experience of most Western Christians. In what way are we called to suffer for our Lord?

A church which is truly part of the body of Christ will suffer in a number of ways. It will be reproached for its evangelism, it will attract those in difficulty and will learn to share their pain, it will minister to the sick and feel their sorrow and uncertainty, it will comfort the bereaved and help them bear their grief, it will have a certain moral integrity which may make its members unpopular in today's society. Its ministers will bear the added burden of spiritual responsibility, a burden which, if not understood by others, may ultimately crush and emasculate their ministry.

'The word of the cross is folly to those who are perishing' (1 Cor. 1.18). Anyone who belongs to a church which takes Christ's call to evangelism seriously, will soon discover that it is not a popular message. We shall lose some friends (The trouble with Woolmer is that he's always trying to convert me!), we shall anger others (Oh, you're so narrow!). We shall face ridicule (a dedicated Christian teacher braves the scorn of colleagues, and the amused mockery of the children, to bring the gospel to his school). We shall be accused of intolerance and of all sorts of strange things. We live in a pluralistic, permissive society, so we are constantly told, which means, in theory, that we can propagate any views we like. But increasingly the cross divides and provokes. It is acceptable if the cross points to one way amongst many, but when we claim that it is the only way, then we are accused of preaching virtual racism.

It may seem strange to list moral integrity as a potential cause of suffering for the Christian. But increasingly, Christians are having to challenge work ethics at a cost to themselves. A girl in our congregation checked the books for a large firm, exposed an internal fraud, and soon afterwards was sacked. Coincidence? Perhaps, but I doubt it. A Christian businessman discovered that his potential foreign customers expected an evening of high-class entertainment with certain sexual diversions laid on. He refused, with some risk of losing both the order and his job. A Christian organization discovers that to get books into a certain country requires customs officers to be bribed. Does the Christian salve his own conscience and refuse, or compromise and make sure that the much-needed literature arrives?

Not all Christians approve of everything Mary Whitehouse does, but there is no doubt that her courage keeps standards on TV, in the theatre, and the video market from slipping even further. She suffers a great deal of personal abuse, and is greatly misunderstood even by her fellow Christians.

The film *Chariots of Fire* tells of the Olympic athlete Eric Liddell's stand on the question of sports on the Sabbath. He earned much vilification for this Christian stand, and he didn't become a hero until he won a different race, run on a different day.

It takes great courage for the Christian leader to enforce church discipline. Just once have I applied the discipline of temporary excommunication. It was done quickly, and only those most closely involved knew that this had happened, but it proved highly beneficial.

Baptismal discipline is highly unpopular and usually misunderstood. In the end it is probably not up to the minister to judge other people's beliefs, but it certainly is his duty to proclaim clearly what baptism means, and what is expected of those who bring their children to the font.

In these and other matters, we must 'bear one another's burdens' (Gal. 6.2). The Christian who takes a moral stand in the outside world will need the prayers and support of his church, and the minister who takes a firm line on discipline will need the support and understanding of his church leaders. All of us, in whatever way we suffer, need to remember the words of St Peter:

> Beloved, do not be surprised at the fiery ordeal which comes upon you to prove you, as though something strange were happening to you. But rejoice in so far as you share Christ's sufferings, that you may also rejoice and be glad when his glory is revealed. If you are reproached for the name of Christ, you are blessed, because the spirit of glory and of God rests upon you (1 Pet. 4.12–14).

Peter knew this well. He had seen the Master come down from the Mount of Transfiguration, with the Spirit of glory clearly resting upon him. He had seen him set his face to Jerusalem to suffer and to die. He had probably seen the young martyr Stephen with the Spirit of glory resting upon him, and he knew that he, too, in God's time must drink the same cup.

Many twentieth-century saints are being persecuted for their faith even as these words are being written. We must neither forget those of our brethren who suffer overseas, nor those who suffer in our midst. A small part of our calling is to forgo some of our ease, and sit alongside them in their time of trial.

Ministering to those with deep problems can be very costly to those who undertake it. The local church will need to learn to share burdens in this respect. A Christian household, or a family, may take a disturbed person into the home. Such a decision cannot be undertaken lightly; the consequences are often horrific. I have seen a number of people virtually destroyed by trying to help those in real difficulties. They get accused of all sorts of failings, and frequently their help is flung back in their face. Yet this is precisely what the gospel calls us to do, and the joy when there is a real change is very wonderful.

Of course, many people's problems are less obvious but no less real. The strain on the single parent, the anxious path of the battered wife, the loneliness of the single and divorced, the hopelessness of the long-term unemployed, all of these are common problems in today's society. Caring people in a church fellowship can provide practical help which may ease the burden. In particular we need to be sensitive in the use of our homes. We need to remember Jesus' words (Luke 14.12–14) about inviting those to our home who will not be able to invite us back.

In our own home, we've never had anyone to stay for a long period (I personally think that just now our family is too young and I'm out too much for this to be practical) but we've sought to help many people in real difficulties. From time to time we've received menacing phone calls, usually after anti-occult ministry. At one time they were so frequent that I started to answer the phone with a tape of Christian music or a cry of 'Merry Christmas' – to the astonishment of some of my genuine callers! Once, threats turned to violence. It was a pretty frightening experience, and one that might have been far worse but for the prayers and physical protection of others. The whole family was so upset that we moved out for a few days.

Ministering to the sick is a bitter-sweet experience. Sweet, because so often they are grateful, and helped by prayer. Sweet, because so often their unselfish faith transcends their pain. Bitter, because so much suffering is debilitating and sickening. Visiting cancer patients, except in those fairly rare cases where prayer or medicine conquers the disease, can be a deeply depressing experience. The steady decline of body, mind and will is hard to see, and hard to minister to. At such times, one feels angry and helpless. And profoundly grateful that our Lord walked a path of suffering and warned us to expect the same.

The way in which many people cope with incurable illness is deeply impressive. The walk, witness and lifestyle of Joni Earickson, an American paraplegic, has been an inspiration to many through her books *Joni* and *One Step Further*. I've valued immensely the friendship of some who have been chronically ill. As I write now their faces smile at me – their work is done, and now they reign with Christ.

There is something awesome about visiting the deathbed of a Christian. A bishop, in a sermon in St Aldate's, told how he used to visit an old lady regularly. Eventually she grew ill and sank into a coma. He came in for a final prayer. Suddenly, she sat up and cried out, 'Jesus, my Lord!' and immediately died. An unforgettable privilege for the minister.

There is something very wonderful, too, about a Christian funeral. It has always been one of the high points of my work. The sense of uplift, of the Lord's own presence, of grief observed and yet overlaid with joy, of gratitude for God's grace, all combine to make such funerals times of worship and rejoicing. The contrast between such occasions and others where the funeral is a necessary routine is very marked. I must confess that I find such occasions very difficult, and yet those too do bring comfort and can really help the relatives.

Bereavement sometimes brings people to faith. A girl in a youth group was killed in a cycling accident. Her faith, and the noticeable change in her lifestyle since becoming a Christian, had been seen by her mother. The care and the witness of her friends, the proclamation of the resurrection at the funeral, all helped to bring her mother gradually and thoughtfully to faith. She became a regular worshipper in the church to which her daughter had belonged.

By contrast, suffering can chill the most radiant faith. C.S. Lewis in *A Grief Observed* wrote of the appalling struggle which he had to continue to believe after his wife's death. For him, suffering did not lead him closer to God. For a while, he was in dark despair, and only gradually did the Divine Light penetrate his soul's gloom.

A recently published book, *My Path of Prayer*, includes a number of examples of how individual Christians have coped with this sort of grief. In it, Edward England makes a most helpful comment:

How does one pray when the eyes are filled with tears? . . . In those dark days of loss, anxiety, self-pity, and unanswered questions, I made a discovery. *I didn't have to pray*. No preacher, no book, had ever told me that. God's love, his understanding, his companionship, were not dependent on my prayers. In these special circumstances I didn't have to seek him – he was there. 'Talk to me again, when you're ready,' he seemed to say, 'I'll be waiting and listening.'

His grief was healed partly by this realization, and partly by a new experience of praise. He had recently published a cassette by the Fisherfolk called *Sound of Living Waters*. This music lifted his gloom and brought spiritual comfort.

None of us knows how we, personally, will react in the face of personal suffering or loss. It is as well to consider these matters before they happen, not in a fatalistic way, but in the realization that they are part of our calling.

All of this can raise great intellectual questions. Indeed, the problem of suffering is the thorniest intellectual problem for the Christian apologist. Scripture never really answers the question 'Why?'. Jesus' only recorded comment on the question – concerning the Tower of Siloam (Luke 13.4) whose fall killed eighteen people – was: 'Do you think they were worse offenders than all the others who dwelt in Jerusalem? I tell you, No; but unless you repent you will all likewise perish.'

The natural disaster is a warning to us that life may be short, and that no one has a right to expect 'three score years and ten'. The writer of Ecclesiastes is reduced to almost total despair by the question:

> Again I saw that under the sun, the race is not to the swift, nor the battle to the strong, nor bread to the wise, nor riches to the intelligent, nor favour to men of skill; but time and chance happens to them all. For a man does not know his time. Like fish that are taken in an evil net, and like birds which are caught in a snare, so the sons of men are snared at an evil time, when it suddenly falls upon them. (Eccl. 9.11,12).

But he was writing without the example of Christ, or the real hope of the resurrection.

It is in the resurrection that we get a glimpse of God's answer. Suffering is not to be avoided, not to be argued about, but to be accepted and endured as part of life's experience. Jesus' life is our great beacon of light. We may not have intellectual answers, but we worship a Lord who has suffered for us and continues to suffer with us. It is surely significant that the heavenly voice said to Saul of Tarsus: 'Saul, Saul, why do you persecute me?' (Acts 9.4) – not 'Why do you persecute my Church?'. This assurance is well expressed in the song,[1]

> 'I walk with you, my children, through valleys filled with gloom;
> In echoes of the starlight and shadows of the moon.
> In the whispers of the night wind are gentle words for you,
> To touch you and assure you it's my world you're walking through.
>
> My love for you, my children, puts rainbows in your hand,

Born of clouded sorrows in a sunburst morning land;
They arch above the smiling eyes where tears can still be seen,
And adorn with gentle trembling touch the bride who is my own.'

St Paul well understood these sentiments, when after writing about present suffering (Rom. 8.18ff), and the groans of creation, he came to the conclusion that: 'Neither death, nor life, nor angels, nor principalities, nor things present, nor things to come, nor powers, nor height, nor depth, nor anything else in all creation, will be able to separate us from the love of God in Christ Jesus our Lord' (Rom. 8.38–9).

NOTE

1 From *Fresh Sounds* by Betty Pulkingham (Hodder & Stoughton 1976).

14 *Training*

'What you have heard from me before many witnesses entrust to faithful men who will be able to teach others also.' (2 Tim. 2.2)

These words from one of Paul's last letters to his most faithful followers sum up thirty years of Christian experience. Paul sensed that he had 'fought the good fight, finished the race, and kept the faith' (2 Tim. 4.6). He knew that his own life and ministry were drawing to an end; his last great concern was that the work should continue. Timothy was one of the standard bearers – one on whom much would depend.

There is a basic Christian principle of growth. As each disciple learns from others, so also he seeks to hand his knowledge on; thus establishing a chain of learning and teaching which extends throughout Christian history. 'What you have heard from me . . . entrust to faithful men.' What had Timothy learnt from Paul? What was the essential core of the faith that he, in his turn, must pass on to others? The experience of Christ! Nothing mattered to Paul more than this, nothing gave him greater courage in the face of hardship and difficulty. 'I know whom I have believed.' (2 Tim. 1.12) Paul had seen Christ in others, he'd met Christ in visions, he'd experienced Christ in daily prayer and in living. He'd seen the touch of Christ as he ministered to others. It was this experience that he counted above all others. 'Indeed I count everything as loss because of the surpassing worth of knowing Christ Jesus my Lord' (Phil. 3.8).

This experience gave Paul a certainty of belonging to God's family. 'You have received the Spirit of sonship. When we cry "Abba! Father!" it is the Spirit himself bearing witness with our spirit that we are children of God . . .' (Rom. 8.15, 16). This certainty was Paul's security. It gave him courage in the face of suffering, setbacks, and impending execution.

Paul's experience of Christ had begun long ago. It had almost certainly been a profoundly disturbing one. He had seen a young man, on trial before the Sanhedrin, gazing upwards with his face shining like the face of an angel (Acts 6.15). The young man's death had been just as impressive. He had argued eloquently from the Scriptures (and that would have appealed to Paul), he had remained calm in the face of insult and attack, his face had continued to shine as he talked of a heavenly vision, and he had prayed for his executioners. Although Saul of Tarsus didn't like to admit it, he had been disturbed. And like many others when disturbed, he had launched a ferocious counter-attack on this pestilential new sect. He, personally, had invaded their houses and dragged people off to prison. And then he had set out for Damascus to seek out any Christians who had infiltrated the synagogues there.

On the way, he was struck blind by a brilliant light. He heard the voice of the risen Lord, he was left sightless and helpless for three days. Eventually, Ananias, a believer who lived in Damascus, had a vision which instructed him to go to a certain road, to a particular house, to pray for one Saul of Tarsus. Not surprisingly, Ananias questioned the vision, but then went in obedience, laid his hands upon Saul, and he received his sight. Ananias doubtless gave him the warning about suffering (Acts 9.16), then he was baptized and ate for the first time for three days.

This experience was followed some time later by the great vision of 2 Corinthians 12.1–5. Here Paul describes how he was caught up into the 'third heaven', and saw things which he could not disclose. Heaven was very real to Paul. He longed to be with Christ (Phil. 1.23), but realized that his work on earth wasn't finished. He appreciated Isaiah's dream of the future life: 'What no eye has seen, nor ear heard, nor the heart of man conceived, what God has prepared for those who love him' (1 Cor. 2.9, quoted from Isa. 64.4). Paul knew that the earthly race was over and that a 'crown of righteousness' was laid up for him in heaven (2 Tim. 4.8).

Paul had other visions. Guidance from the man of Macedonia (Acts 16.9), warning from the Holy Spirit of troubles in Jerusalem (21.11), comfort from an angel during the storm at sea, on the way to Rome (27.23). He had many other evidences of God's presence. The blinding of Elymas, the healing of the cripple at Lystra, the earthquake at Philippi, the healings at Ephesus, the raising to life of Eutychus, the healing of Publius' father in Malta, were just a few of the signs and wonders which he witnessed.

But what was it that kept Paul's experience of Christ so fresh and real? It cannot just have been revelations (he specifically warned the Colossians against this – Col. 2.18) or signs and wonders (which could be a mark of the opposition – 2 Thess. 2.9). Almost certainly it was his prayer life. He doesn't tell us much about it, he doesn't give us experience of prayer meetings – except the great one at Antioch when in response to prophecy the missionary journey of Paul and Barnabas was begun (Acts 13.1–3) – but he does pray.

He remembered Timothy constantly in his prayers (2 Tim. 1.3), he remembered Philemon thankfully (Philem. 4), he prayed without ceasing for the Romans (Rom. 1.9), he joyfully remembered the Philippians (Phil. 1.4), he prayed gratefully for the Colossians (whom he had never met! Col. 1.3), and he prayed very specifically for the Ephesians. Paul's written prayers helped to train others in the vital work of prayer.

It is worth quoting in full his two great prayers for the Ephesians:

For this reason, because I have heard of your faith in the Lord Jesus and your love toward all the saints, I do not cease to give thanks for you, remembering you in my prayers, that the God of our Lord Jesus Christ, the Father of glory, may give you a spirit of wisdom and of revelation in the knowledge of him, having the eyes of your hearts enlightened, that you may know what is the hope to which he has called you, what are the riches of his glorious inheritance in the saints, and what is the immeasurable greatness of his power in us who believe, according to the working of his great might which he accomplished in Christ when he raised him from the dead and made him sit at his right hand in the heavenly places, far above all rule and authority and power and dominion, and above every name that is named, not only in this age but also in that which is to come; and he has put all things under his feet and has made him the head over all things for the church, which is his body, the fullness of him who fills all in all (Eph. 1.15–23).

For this reason I bow my knees before the Father, from whom every family in heaven and on earth is named, that according to the riches of his glory he may grant you to be strengthened with might through his spirit in the inner man, and that Christ may dwell in your hearts through faith; that you being rooted and grounded in love, may have power to comprehend with all the saints what is the breadth and length and height and depth, and to know the love of Christ which surpasses knowledge, that you may be filled with all the fullness of God. Now to him who by the power at work within us is able to do far more abundantly than all that we ask or think, to him be glory in the church and in Christ Jesus to all generations, for ever and ever. Amen (Eph. 3.14–21).

In the first prayer, Paul remembered gratefully their progress in the faith, and he asked especially for wisdom and revelation. This would be especially necessary in view of his own revelation given to them in his farewell speech (Acts 20.29) that fierce wolves would come amongst them. He prays that they may have a clear understanding of the future hope, and more experience of God's power in the present. The prayer ends with a crescendo of praise to God the Father.

In his next prayer, he continues to pray that they may have a real and deep experience of God's love. He dares to ask that they may experience the fullness of God. His final sentence of praise (often used by modern preachers without much hope at the end of a dry sermon), reminds them, and us, how important the Church is to God.

One can feel Paul's spirit rising as he writes these great prayers. Although a prisoner for the Lord, an ambassador in chains, he can approach the throne of grace with confidence and praise.

How exciting it is when we, applying Paul's teaching, experience something of these things. We, too, sense God's presence in our prayer times. When we obey Jesus' specific command (Matt. 6.6) to close the door and to pray secretly to our father in heaven, our spirits rise and our days go better. When we forget this discipline, we relapse into frantic, and usually unprofitable, discipleship. We will never be great pray-ers in public, still less prophets or preachers, if we don't use the secret times to be alone with God. Sometimes in my bachelor days, I used to fret if I wasn't invited out on a Saturday night. Yet those evenings became precious times, when I could give plenty of time to the Scriptures and to prayer. These times, for all of us, are like the hidden part of the iceberg, preparing us for the public ministry that will follow on.

How marvellous, too, is that 'spirit of wisdom and revelation'! What Paul prayed for the Ephesians, can be experienced by us today. I never cease to wonder when I see this happening. Sometimes, in the public healing ministry, gifted pray-ers sense exactly what is wrong with people and what God wants to heal. Sometimes, in private ministry a revelation confirms or exposes God's plan.

I remember once taking someone to pray in a house that was disturbed. The woman who lived there was suffering from bad dreams. About a year earlier she had suffered a bad experience from a lodger who was a confidence trickster. He left suddenly (and was never heard of again), leaving financial chaos, and a sense of spiritual deceit. Looking back i feel that I failed him – he professed conversion and apparently renounced an occult past. I anointed him with oil, he shook badly and said it burnt him. I feel that I didn't spend sufficient time with him after that and that the experience probably encouraged him to run away (which we discovered afterwards that he regularly did). Anyway, nothing could or can be done (unless by the grace of God, he reads these pages!). I prepared to pray when my companion said, 'Look up Zechariah 5.4.' 'I will send it forth, says the Lord of hosts, and it shall enter the house of the thief, and the house of him who swears falsely by my name; and it shall abide in his house and consume it, both timber and stones.' I doubt whether there is a verse in the whole of Scripture which more accurately could have summed up the feeling of evil left by that man's influence! At that time, my praying partner was troubled by a deep and trying personal problem. Not long afterwards she prayed through the night saying to the Lord, 'If you can give me revelations for others, can you give them for myself?' Eventually a strange answer came, but when others prayed with her along those lines the problem lifted.

The sense of uplift and joy at these times of spiritual release is indescribable. I can recall many times (and I'm not a great one for praise sessions!) after ministry, being lifted heavenward, as we rejoiced in the extraordinary graciousness of God. This sense of praise is also especially present after healing services and at the end of missions. Time and time again, at the end of such services there would be an ongoing spirit of worship and adoration. I remember leaving one healing service after much ministry, while the congregation were dancing and praising the Lord. I also remember a Good News Crusade at Blaithwaite in Cumbria when, despite mud and rain, there was praise and joy. A thousand or more in a tent giving glory to God, and then hushed to receive a word of prophecy, or experience one of the leaders with a gift of knowledge for someone's healing, was wonderful. Several people even claimed to have heard angels singing one night.

These special times of God's blessing are essential moments of upbuilding to teach us and keep us faithful for the battle ahead. Remembrance of God's past blessing helps us to trust him for the future.

Paul was no stranger to disappointment and discouragement. Yet at these times, as well, he was able to remain faithful and steadfast. This utter realism is a vital experience which Paul needed to pass on to those he sought to train. The Galatian churches were a great disappointment to him. He had preached so freely (Acts 13.13—15.2; and 16.1–5). He had left the new churches (Acts 16.5) in a strong and encouraging state. They had seen signs and wonders. They knew what it meant to be led by the Spirit. But Paul soon had to write to them with stern words: 'O foolish Galatians! Who has bewitched you . . . Did you receive the Spirit by works of the law, or by hearing with faith? . . . Did you experience so many things in vain . . . .?' (Gal. 3.1–5).

It was a heart-breaking experience. Legalistic Jewish Christians who had appeared at the end of Paul's first missionary journey (Acts 15.1), whose views had been rejected by the Apostolic Council in Jerusalem (Acts 15), had started preaching a perverted gospel of faith plus obedience to the ceremonial law. This was one of many dark nights for Paul. His final letter to Timothy hints of others. The Christians in the province of Asia have rejected him (and perhaps the Lord? 2 Tim. 1.15); Hymaenus and Phygelus (2.17) are teaching heresy about the resurrection; false teachers are upsetting weak women (3.6); Demas, 'in love with this world', has deserted him (4.10); other friends are doing good work elsewhere. Only Luke remained with him. One bright spot is Paul's desire to see Mark (4.11). Mark's desertion on the first journey (Acts 13.13) had led to Paul's quarrel with Barnabas at the beginning of the next journey (Acts 15.36–40). It is good to know that this difference had been settled, and that Paul now respected Mark's work.

We shall all have our own particular dark nights. It is part of the experience of testing and growth that God seems to require of us all. It is part of the pruning process designed to make us more dependent upon God and less upon ourselves. One friend who had been through a long dark patch after leaving our church told me that he'd always doubted me when I'd preached about this. Now he understood what I meant, and had been grateful for the warning.

The other inevitable experience for Paul was physical suffering. 'Do not be ashamed then of testifying to our Lord, nor of me his prisoner, but share in suffering for the gospel in the power of God' (2 Tim. 1.8).

Paul's experience of suffering was very real. Writing to the Corinthians at a time when they were challenging his authority and his teaching, he reminds them of his suffering for the gospel (2 Cor. 11.24–9). He has been beaten many times, stoned and left for dead (cf. Acts 14.19), faced frequent natural disasters from shipwrecks, rivers, wildernesses, etc., he has met human opposition from Jews, from Gentiles, from robbers, from false brethren, and above all that there is the daily anxiety about the state of the churches.

This was his greatest worry. Dangers came and went, but the fortunes of the churches were less easily mended. Any pastor, or lay leader, knows the thrill when things are going well, and the bleak despair when they aren't. Paul had plenty of each experience. He had one great skill – he could take any opportunity. An unexpected arrival in Malta gave him a chance to work there, and even in prison he spread the gospel amongst the guards (Phil. 1.13) and led to faith the runaway slave Onesimus.

Another essential quality that Timothy must have learnt from Paul was faithfulness. This faithfulness involved training. 'I do not run aimlessly . . . but I pommel my body and subdue it, lest after preaching to others, I myself should be disqualified' (1 Cor. 9.26). Training did not involve only bodily exercise (1 Tim. 4.8). More importantly it involved the pursuit of godliness. Faithfulness meant hard work. Paul commended the hard-working farmer (2 Tim. 2.6), Proverbs commended the hard-working ant (Prov. 6.6–8), Jesus commended the faithful and hardworking servants who were ready for the Master's return (Luke 12.35–40).

Faithfulness also meant singlemindedness. The soldier on active service (2 Tim. 2.4) avoids civilian distractions. God's soldiers must not be deflected from their chosen calling. Probably one of the greatest dangers today is that local church leaders get so involved in committees, fund-raising, social events, and so on, that they seldom go out on to the front lines and really seek the lost. It is fatally easy to be distracted from the real work, and then one wonders why there is so little harvest.

The faithful teacher must also set a personal example. Paul was never embarrassed to draw attention to himself: 'Now you have observed my conduct' (2 Tim. 3.10, also Acts 20.20). Timothy could learn from Paul, and then others could learn from Timothy. And what was Timothy going to teach his hearers? A number of things – sound words, avoiding irrelevant distractions, urgency, and Scripture. Timothy was to use the Scriptures (2 Tim. 3.16) as the basis of his work. They were his textbook, his means of correction, and his training manual. Sound words meant that the word of truth had to be rightly handled (2.15). Inessentials were to be avoided. Paul cites elegant discussions over the meanings of words as one example of wasting God's time. Yet how often our Bible studies and sermons are little more than that!

There is a great sense of urgency in Paul's writings. Timothy was to preach the word in season and out of season (2 Tim. 4.2). It is fatally easy for all of us to go 'off duty'. Even days off, much needed though they are, may provide opportunities for preaching the word. And how was Timothy to teach others? Paul doesn't outline any training scheme for Timothy. But the aim was clear: Timothy was to teach others so that they, in their turn, could pass on the word. The gospel was never to be static; each learner was also to become a teacher.

One of the most exciting things at St Aldate's was our lay training course[1]. Ultimately, we shared this with several other churches. It had many aims and covered a wide range of topics: personal spirituality, the basis of the gospel, sharing one's faith, leading groups, counselling . . . It led to some surprising results. Not least when one PCC member tried in a group exercise to share the basis of his faith, only to discover that in no real sense had he entered the L-shaped field. His conversion revolutionized the end of his working life and he ended up in full-time service in the Church. Often the counselling exercises opened up real problems and led to undreamt of progress and freedom for the participants.

But best of all were the experiences gained from 'active service'. Parish weekends, small missions, public speaking all provided real opportunities for growth. I remember, in particular, one weekend in the Midlands with a group from St

Matthew's. We went to a marvellous church. This was a great help, as sometimes the missions foundered because the places we went to really weren't ready to receive what was said. On the final Sunday afternoon we were greatly encouraged when over seventy people turned up, either to learn about healing or to be prayed for for a new release in the Spirit. The evening service was amazing. Some of our team used spiritual gifts that they had never been able to share in public before, there was a great cutting free from occult bondage, some were converted (although the weekend didn't have an evangelistic aim!), and more sought healing and special prayer. There was great joy in the congregation. We drove back, tired and late at night, feeling that we had experienced one of the best weekends of our lives!

Training is an ongoing necessity. In St Matthew's, as in many churches, lay people read the first part of the communion service, sometimes preach, lead the prayers, share in the post-communion prayer ministry. They lead fellowship groups in their homes, quite often lead the prayer meeting, as well as doing all the normal things like running youth organizations, tending the church grounds, repairing the plant, and keeping an eye on the elderly. They also launched out, with very little help from me, on door-to-door visiting. The leaders meet fort-nightly for breakfast, bringing the whole family, and rotating around one another's houses. There are many more things which need doing – more contact with other churches (especially the Asian church), visiting of Asians, some project with the unemployed, more help for the single parent. Obviously with small numbers, about 100 adults, there is a limit to the amount that can be achieved. But only as each person is enabled to grow and find his own place in the body will the church fulfil its potential. Different people have different gifts. The practical contribution of some, say by cleaning the hall or running the crèche, may seem less spectacular than visiting or preaching, yet each is just as necessary for the welfare of the whole.

People need encouragement to exercise their prayer gifts. At a conference I was very unwell, and after one session about twenty people wanted prayer. I asked a number of the other leaders to help in this prayer time. They were inexperienced but afterwards were very grateful, having learnt much from step-ping out in faith.

I was grateful to Fred Smith when, just before I left Oxford, he left me one evening in charge of his congregation. People seemed to be healed and blessed, just as if he was present. It was the same Lord using a different channel!

A good leader will train others and begin to work himself out of a job. A good house group leader will train others in leadership, so that when the group grows and splits, natural leaders will have emerged. A good disciple, however young and timid in the faith, will look for others.

Which brings us to Paul's great injunction to Timothy (2 Tim. 1.6,7). 'Hence I remind you to rekindle the gift of God that is within you through the laying on of my hands; for God did not give us a spirit of timidity but a spirit of power and love and self-control.' Effective training will depend upon this gift. If we are timid, we will fail to teach and to rebuke – we will mumble half-truths and platitudes. If we lack self-control, we shall crumple under persecution and disappointment. If we lack love, we are nothing; our example will put off rather than attract. If we lack power, the necessary signs and encouragements will be missing. We need to pray for those we train, with faith and expectation. We need to pray for them to receive the fullness of the Spirit's empowering, and for full protection for them from the assaults of the enemy. We need to train them to work in small groups and not as individuals.

Jesus rejoiced greatly when the seventy returned (Luke 10.1–24) having seen great things. We shall rejoice greatly as those whom we have been privileged to train flower into effective discipleship. We want our disciples not only to move towards the centre of the L-shaped field, but to teach others how to follow them there.

NOTE

1   Details of SALT are available from St Aldate's Church, Oxford.

Postscript

A few years ago, Jane, Rachel (then aged two), and I were picnicking in a wood in the south of France. It was a very hot day and we were glad to sit in the shade. I glanced up and noticed several large dark butterflies flapping about on the branch of an oak tree. My heart missed a beat – surely they were Large Tortoiseshells? This butterfly, rare or extinct in England, had always eluded me. Then I looked up the main tree trunk and there, alongside a clump of ivy, one was gently opening and closing its wings. The unusual quantity of the butterflies, and their lazy uncertain flight, suggested that they were just emerged from the chrysalis. I stood happily and watched.

Then disaster struck. A hornet flew into the wood and, as if guided by radar, made straight for the butterfly, sat astride its body, and pierced its wings. Four fragile wings fluttered down and fell at my feet. Moments later, I noticed yet another Tortoiseshell cautiously opening and shutting its wings. It was just inches away from the hornet. Would it, too, be devoured? Jane and I threw earth and stones at the tree trunk. Eventually Jane landed a hit on the tree trunk just below the insects. Butterfly and hornet flew off in opposite directions!

Earlier, in our camp site, I had witnessed the roles reversed. For several days, a Red Admiral lived in our rectangle. It fed off the sweet flowering hedges, and often rested on our car roof, much to the delight of Rachel. Once it saw a hornet flying menacingly across its territory. With an angry flap of its big black wings it took off and flew round and round the hornet. The hornet, alarmed, turned and sought food elsewhere.

'Be sober, be watchful. Your adversary the devil prowls around like a roaring lion, seeking someone to devour. Resist him, firm in your faith . . .' (1 Pet. 5.8). That in a way sums up the message of this book. Both butterflies had experienced the miracle of rebirth; using the introductory metaphor, both had entered the L-shaped field. The Tortoiseshell, however, never quite had the faith to fly and it was cut down before it could be any use. And that is one of Satan's prime tactics. If he cannot prevent our rebirth, he will try to limit our usefulness, he will try to prevent us growing up into salvation. We are only dangerous, from his point of view, as we start bearing fruit, thirty-fold, sixty-fold, a hundred-fold.

It is of course fatally easy for the disciple to cease to 'fly', and just to sit, idly flapping wings, in the shade. Paul experienced this with the Galatian church (see Chapter 14 of this book) when they relapsed from faith to law. It can easily happen to us. We join a live church, enjoy the sermons and the worship, but sit back and cease to grow; or we find ourselves in a hostile environment and give up attempting to walk by faith. In these situations, we are an easy target for the enemy, who may simply choose to leave us sleeping rather than attack directly. 'Save some by snatching them out of the fire' (Jude 23). Our tactics to save the second Large Tortoiseshell were somewhat desperate, but at least they worked! The stone drove away the hornet, and stirred the butterfly into flight.

Young Christians sometimes need this desperate sort of ministry. The time just after the new birth is a vital period. It is fatally easy to lapse back into the old ways, particularly for those who have come with some deep problem, say from depression, alcohol, or some form of spiritual darkness. There is a special vulnerability. But if established Christians remain alert, and watch over their progress, very soon they will grow into sufficient faith to be able (inasmuch as any of us can!), to fly and look after themselves.

'Now to him who is able to keep you from falling' (Jude 24). We have, in Christ, victory over Satan. The hornet can be resisted and driven away. With the flight of faith, wearing the armour of Christ, we can see great things. It is Christ's intention that, as we grow up to salvation, so we shall experience the thrill of a victorious Christian life. Through worship, at prayer, in ministry, with the friendship of others, we shall learn something of the greatness of our God.

As we leave the shadows of the edge of the field, or the false safety of the tree, and as we move towards the centre, we shall discover that we are not alone. Not only is he with us, but countless of his friends are alongside. And as we grow up to salvation, so the wonder of God's miracle – our rebirth – will increase. And as that wonder increases, the step of our discipleship will grow firmer. Let John Bunyan's pilgrim have the final word:

Who would true valour see,
Let him come hither;
One here will constant be,
Come wind, come weather;
There's no discouragement
Shall make him once relent
His first avowed intent
To be a pilgrim.

Whoso beset him round
With dismal stories,
Do but themselves confound;
His strength the more is.
No lion can him fright;
He'll with a giant fight,
But he will have the right
To be a pilgrim.

No goblin nor foul fiend
Can daunt his spirit;
He knows he at the end
Shall life inherit.
Then, fancies fly away;
He'll not fear what men say;
He'll labour night and day
To be a pilgrim.